THE BRIDE WORE CRIMSON

AND OTHER STORIES

Bryan Woolley

*For Jim Wieck,
Good friend —
Bryan Woolley*

THE BRIDE WORE CRIMSON

AND

OTHER

STORIES

by

Bryan

Woolley

TEXAS WESTERN PRESS
THE UNIVERSITY OF TEXAS AT EL PASO

Copyright © 1993
Texas Western Press
The University of Texas at El Paso
El Paso, Texas 79968-0633

All rights reserved. No part of this book may be used or reproduced in any manner without written permission from Texas Western Press, except in the case of brief quotations employed in reviews and similar critical works.

First Edition
Library of Congress Catalog
  Card No. 92-061947
ISBN 0-87404-227-5
ISBN 0-87404-228-3

∞ All Texas Western Press books are printed on acid-free paper, meeting the guidelines for permanence and durability of the Committee on Production Guidelines for Book Longevity of the Council on Library Resources.

Nearly all the stories in this book originally appeared in *The Dallas Morning News* and its magazine, *Dallas Life*, some of them in a slightly altered form. "Glory Denied" as it appears here was published in *Nova*, but another version was in the *Morning News*. "West Texas" was published originally in *Westways*. I thank the publishers for permission to reprint my work here, and my friend Mike Maza for coming up with the title of the lead piece, which also became the title of the book.

Again,

For Isabel

It's all I have to bring today -
This, and my heart beside ...
Emily Dickinson

CONTENTS

1.... THE BRIDE WORE CRIMSON

17 .... THE HANDS AND EYE OF TEXAS BILLY MAYS

29 .... WHERE HAVE ALL THE HORNY TOADS GONE?

35 .... THE DEATH OF AUSTIN SQUATTY

43 .... TRUCKING

53 .... FREEDOM FIGHTERS

63 .... JOHN

75 .... THE $65,000 FISH STORY

85 .... TOWER AMONG FRIENDS

97 .... A FAMILY NIGHTMARE

117 .... GLORY DENIED

127 .... BECAUSE IT'S STILL HERE

133 .... THE REAL PEPPER-UPPER

139 .... MEMORIES OF SELMA

151 .... GOING WITH THE DAWGS

161 .... HANGING IN

173 .... THE YEAR OF RECONCILIATION

181 .... OLD FRIENDS

191 ....: WEST TEXAS

INTRODUCTION

Nobody can upstage Molly Ivins's wonderful story in her introduction to his *The Edge of the West* (Texas Western Press, 1990), of having "waltzed across Texas" with Bryan Woolley in the *Dallas Times Herald* newsroom on the day Ernest Tubb died, but I did sit next to Bryan on the evening he taught Louis L'Amour a lesson about writing Western novels.

We were in Branson, Missouri, late in June, 1984, at the convention of Western Writers of America, Inc. This organization of 500 writers of novels and nonfiction works on the American West gives an award, called the Golden Spur, at its annual gathering, for the best Western novel, historical novel, short story, magazine article, juvenile work and movie and television script. The Spur is the Oscar of the Western writing world, and Bryan had been nominated for the award for his novel *Sam Bass*.

Among his competitors in the historical novel category was the redoubtable Louis Dearborn L'Amour, author of upwards of a hundred Western novels which had sold the equivalent of two or three copies for every man, woman, child and family pet in the United States, whose books were published by the prestigious Bantam Books of New York, who had appeared on "60 Minutes," who had received a Congressional Gold Medal, a Presidential Medal of Freedom, a Buffalo Bill Award, two American Book Awards, four honorary LL.Ds and, more than likely, a Six Maids a-Milking and a Partridge in a Pear Tree award from somebody.

"I haven't got a shot at this," Bryan told me as we found our Spur banquet seats that Thursday evening of the last day of the Branson convention. "*Louis L'Amour?*" he said. The unspoken part of this threnody was "Why *this* year? Why *me?*"

L'Amour's nominated book, *The Lonesome Gods*, a more mystical novel, and a fatter one, than his readers-by-the-legions were accustomed to, had been elegantly jacketed and lavishly promoted by Bantam and had been warmly received by reviewers across the country.

Bryan's *Sam Bass*, published by the respectable but obscure Corona Books of San Antonio, had appeared in a grocery sack-like brown jacket, had no promotional money behind it, was well reviewed in Texas but nowhere else.

"*Louis L'Amour?*" Bryan said.

Now, one element that makes the Spur Awards meaningful to those who receive them is that they come as a result of peer-judging -- historical book writers read and judge the history books submitted, novelists read and judge the novels, and so on. And these professionals are not influenced by big names, big promotional efforts, big reviews, colorful dustjackets or anything other than the quality of the book.

Bryan and *Sam Bass* won, easily.

There was a nice extra element, too. The stunned Bryan Woolley accepted his Spur that muggy summer evening in the Ozarks from C.L. "Doc" Sonnichsen, a beloved figure in WWA as he had been at Texas Western College when Bryan was one of his students in the mid-1950s. (In accepting his award, Bryan said, "Everything I know I learned from Doc Sonnichsen.")

In 1974, I reviewed Bryan's first novel, *Some Sweet Day*, for an El Paso newspaper. I had never heard of Bryan Woolley and forget exactly what I said about his book other than that I regarded it (and still do) as among the best of all Texas novels. When we met for the first time a few years later, he reminded me of that review. I said something about how much I admired his *Time and Place* (1977). I discovered he had read a book or two of mine, that he had a passion for Jack London's stories, as I do, and that he remembered books and writers out of his childhood in the Davis Mountain country of West Texas which matched my own list of youthful passions in the flatlands of central Illinois—Edgar Rice Burroughs, John R. Tunis, Harold Lamb, James Oliver Curwood, Jack O'Brien's immortal *Silver Chief, Dog of the North*.

We became friends.

The Branson episode proved something I'd known about Bryan long before he knew, beyond a shadow of a doubt, that he would bow to Louis L'Amour in Branson: He has never known how remarkable it is that he can write novels as memorable as any written in Texas or anywhere else, can write short stories so fine they appear in the best of national magazines, and can write newspaper work of such quality that it has established him as a premiere figure in Texas journalism.

He does not know how good and versatile a writer he is but the proof is in any of his books.

In *The Bride Wore Crimson* we see both the journalist and novelist at work. This is not to say that there is fiction in these Texas pieces, but the *techniques* of fiction are in every one of them: characters we remember long after the story and the book have been read, descriptive lines, color, a sense of time and place, plot (in Woolley's hands, a magazine article is plotted; it is a *story*, after all, even if a true story), pace, suspense, rising and falling action—all the techniques only a novelist can employ successfully.

Small wonder, then, that the title story in this book reads like a vintage murder mystery with all the characters, events and evidence presented for the reader to judge; or that "A Family Nightmare" can leave us so horrified and frustrated; or that in reading his "The Death of Austin Squatty" we are left wondering—but somehow knowing—what happened to that strange and irrepressible Texan, John Jenkins.

John Graves of Glen Rose, Texas, comes to life in Bryan's story as he never has before, even to those who have admired and studied those Texas classics, *Goodbye to a River* and *Hard Scrabble*. The same may be said of the story on the late Senator John Tower and that on the Seminole Scouts.

Even in his lighter pieces, people and things spring to life, as they do in the best of fiction. Shuffleboard *meister* Texas Billy Mays ("He's so wiry he could be mistaken for scrawny," Bryan says of him) is not just a saloon hustler who slides metal weights down a 20-foot-long slab of waxed rock maple, he is a living, breathing and interesting *character*. Those who searched for Tangle-Free Tom in the Lake Texoma Crappiethon have dimension, as does the fish, and the *phrynosoma cornutum* isn't just an ugly little lizard, it is the *Horny Toad*, friends, and you really do get concerned about where they have all gone.

Bryan Woolley is one of my two favorite Texas writers (Elroy Bode of El Paso is the other) and my single best accomplishment as director of Texas Western Press was to be able to publish books by both these splendid writers.

The Bride Wore Crimson is the second of Bryan's books to appear under our imprint. I'm hoping there will be others.

— Dale L. Walker

THE BRIDE WORE CRIMSON

You get a strange feeling when you discover - even half a century after the fact - that your uncle once stood trial for murder, and that the victim was his wife. Such knowledge becomes a burden, and you feel compelled to do something about it. So I'm telling the story.

DOROTHY MARIE WOOLLEY, A BRIDE OF TWO MONTHS AND SIX DAYS, was lounging on her bed in her new honeymoon cottage on Ellsworth Avenue, trying to solve the puzzle posed by "Ripley's Believe It or Not" in the comics section of the Sunday paper:

"There are two volumes of a novel, each two inches thick, with covers one-fourth of an inch thick. If the volumes are upright side by side and a bookworm starts eating on the first page of the first volume and eats straight through to the last page of the second volume, how far will he go?"

It was 9:30 a.m. The breakfast dishes were washed, the garbage had been carried out, the beds had been made. November 5, 1933, was drizzly in Dallas, a good morning to be at home and reading the paper.

Dorothy was a pretty young woman, blond, slender, blue-eyed, just 20 years old. She was dressed as a woman might dress on a Sunday morning when her marriage was still new — a pink teddy, silk stockings, slippers, a delicate pink smock. She was lying on her side, propped on her left elbow, her left hand against her face. Her head was near the foot of the bed. Her feet were resting against the arm of a rocking chair close beside the bed.

Dorothy's sister-in-law, Mina Woolley, also 20 years old, also pretty, was sitting in the rocker, reading another section of the paper. On the other side of the bed, near its foot, Dorothy's husband, Toy Woolley, sat on the vanity bench that had come with their new dresser. He was handsome, blond, blue-eyed and slender, too, and eight years older than his wife and his sister.

Toy was facing away from the bed, holding a shotgun across his lap. It was a new Browning automatic, given to him only the day before by his wife. Dorothy had bought it as a Christmas gift, but she had presented it to him early so he could go hunting with it before the duck season ended.

On the floor beside the bench lay a Remington .22 rifle, Toy's own early Christmas gift to his wife. Near the rifle were a cleaning ramrod, an oil can, and some rags.

The way Toy was holding the shotgun, its barrel protruded back toward the bed under his left arm. Its muzzle was only a couple of feet from Dorothy. With his right hand, Toy was rubbing the gun with a rag.

"It went off," Mina would testify later. "Toy threw the gun down and jumped. As he did this, the back of his knees sent the bench across the room several feet. At first I thought he had shot himself."

But it was Dorothy who had been hit. All the shot and even the wadding of the shotgun shell entered her body just above her heart. The arm that had been propping her collapsed, her head dropped, her blood poured over "Ripley's Believe It or Not."

Toy Woolley was my uncle. I say "was" because he has been dead for quite a few years. But even if he were alive I would say "was." After my parents were divorced, when I was eight years old, I never had contact with my father's side of my family. But I have a few hazy memories of Uncle Toy, and they all have guns in them.

Shotguns, especially. When I was very young, he used to come to our farm in Comanche County to hunt with my father. This was about 10 years after he killed Dorothy. I remember him in the yellowish canvas jacket that hunters wore in those days, with loops across the front to hold shotgun shells. And the shotgun, huge and dark, cradled in his arms.

I also remember a Christmas. World War II was on, and all the metal and rubber was being used in the fight, so our toys under the tree were crude things, made of wood. Santa Claus had brought my brother a wooden tommy gun with a ratchet thing in it, like one of those Halloween noisemakers. You turned a crank, and it made a tommy-gun noise. I remember Uncle Toy picking up that gun, pointing it at me and turning the crank. Then he laughed.

That's all I remember about Uncle Toy. I never heard about him and Dorothy and what happened on Ellsworth Avenue on that Sunday morning before I was born. I don't remember ever meeting Aunt Mina. And I never heard of the "other woman," Mae Cantrell. It wasn't something that the family discussed very often, probably — and never around the children.

Then one day several years ago, I was walking through the newsroom of the *Dallas Times Herald*, and another reporter, Gary Shultz, called my name. "Do you have a relative named Toy Woolley?" he asked.

"I used to. He was my uncle. He's dead now."

"You might be interested in this," Gary said. He handed me a yellowing clip file that he had found deep in a box in a corner of a storeroom. It was the story of the death of Dorothy Marie Woolley, and what happened before and after she died.

Mina ran to the home of William Hidell, a neighbor. "My brother was cleaning his gun," she said. "I think he has killed his wife." Mr. Hidell and his wife returned with her. They found Dorothy lying in her blood on the bed. Toy was holding her head.

"Let's take her to a doctor," Toy said. He laid Dorothy down and went to get his car out of the garage. When he returned, Mr. Hidell met him at the door.

"Dorothy is dead," he said.

Toy collapsed. Mr. Hidell carried him into the house.

"Did his grief seem real to you?" the defense lawyer later would ask him.

"Yes, it was real. He couldn't have been that good an actor."

"Did they get along well with each other?"

"Like a newly married couple. They showed the utmost consideration for each other."

Mina telephoned Dorothy's mother, Esta Joynes, and broke the news. When Mrs. Joynes arrived at the house, Mina and the neighbors begged her not to go into the room where Dorothy lay. But she insisted.

"She was alone there . . . dead . . . lying on the bed," Mrs. Joynes would testify. "It looked to me like she had been shot while she was asleep. Her eyes were closed, and there was a faint smile on her lips. Toy was in the front room. He was raving, but he never shed a tear. He told me it was an accident."

Mrs. Joynes went back to the living room and sat down. Toy knelt in front of her and put his head in her lap. "What am I going to do without Dorothy?" he asked. Mrs. Joynes stroked his hair.

The police had arrived. Toy told them he had been duck hunting in East Texas the day before, and didn't know he had left a shell in the gun. Dr. D.P. Laugenour pronounced Dorothy dead and shot a quarter grain of morphine into Toy's arm to calm him. Justice of the Peace John Baldwin returned a verdict of accidental homicide. An ambulance carried Dorothy away.

Monday morning, Toy went to the funeral home with Mrs. Joynes and her son, Ralph. They chose a casket, and Mrs. Joynes and Ralph signed the note for the funeral bill of $1,037.50. Toy didn't. "He just sat there," the funeral director would testify.

Later that morning, two of Toy's brothers, Lynn and Ray, and James Godfrey, their brother-in-law, accompanied Toy to a florist shop to buy flowers for the funeral, which was to be at 2 p.m. in the living room of the honeymoon cottage. James would say later that he and the brothers took turns watching over the distraught widower all day Monday. "We were afraid he might try to commit suicide because of the accident," he said.

The clerk at the florist shop remembered that one of the brothers had to support Toy while he was in her store, that he was too grief-stricken to choose the flowers he wanted. He left the choice to her.

The men returned to the cottage on Ellsworth Avenue, and Toy's brothers put him to bed. When the hearse brought Dorothy's corpse to the house, about 1:30, Toy got up to look at her.

"He collapsed twice," James said. "We put him back to bed."

He remained there while Dr. L.N.D. Wells, pastor of East Dallas Christian Church, said the last words over Dorothy in the living room, and while the hearse carried her to her grave in Restland Memorial Park.

Mrs. Joynes would testify that on Tuesday, two days after the shooting, Toy was "anxious" about a $1,000 life insurance policy that he recently had taken out on Dorothy.

On Wednesday, during a meeting with Mrs. Joynes and Ralph and his own lawyer, Toy declared that he wouldn't waive any of his legal rights to Dorothy's estate. "He claimed all her cash and estate and an interest in my property," Mrs. Joynes said.

Later that day, she met with her own lawyer and learned to her dismay that since Dorothy had left no will, Toy was entitled to her entire estate, possibly including an interest in Mrs. Joynes' own home.

For a 20-year-old woman in the midst of the Great Depression, Dorothy had been well-fixed. A year before her own death, her father had committed suicide, leaving a note addressed only to her. He also left her a $14,000 life insurance policy and several pieces of real estate, including an interest in the family home. He left his widow less than $3,000. Ralph inherited nothing.

Dorothy had put her money in a trust fund with the insurance company. A week after she and Toy married, they bought their new house on Ellsworth Avenue for $5,650. They paid $3,150 in cash, and signed a note, payable in 30 days, for $2,500. Both the cash and the note were paid from Dorothy's trust fund.

Dorothy also had paid for the car that Toy drove, most of the food they ate, and the shotgun with which Toy killed her. When she died, about $6,000 remained in her trust fund. Her checking account had a balance of about $300.

On Wednesday, Toy met with Mrs. Joynes again. This time he offered to relinquish his interest in two pieces of real estate and give Mrs. Joynes $2,000 if she would give up any claim to the rest of Dorothy's estate.

"I told him I would accept the settlement," Mrs. Joynes said. "The next day, he kissed me and told me he had decided to give me $2,500 in cash instead of $2,000."

But at 1 p.m. that day, when Toy was walking on South Akard Street, a pair of Dallas police detectives approached him, flashed their badges and arrested him. They took him to a room in the Jefferson Hotel, where they and investigators from the district attorney's office questioned him for six hours.

At 7 p.m., they took him to the Dallas County Jail, and at 9 p.m., they charged him with deliberately planning the murder of his wife. District Attorney Bob Hurt wouldn't agree to bond. Toy was locked up.

Two nights earlier, J.J. Cantrell, described in the newspapers as "a wealthy landowner from Comanche County," had telephoned the

Dallas police. He said the shooting of Dorothy Marie Woolley "might have some unpleasant angles" that they should investigate. The police asked him to come to Dallas.

Mr. Cantrell and his daughter, Mae, had arrived Wednesday by bus. He handed over to the police a packet of letters that Toy had written to Mae.

"I don't want to talk to anybody," Toy told the reporters at the jail. "There are lots of things that have got to be straightened out."

Mae Cantrell was born on a farm three miles from the farm where Toy was born, near the tiny community of Lamkin in Comanche County. She was two years younger than Toy. As they grew up, they knew each other well. Indeed, they were first cousins once removed. Toy's grandfather was Mae's uncle.

"Were you sweethearts as boy and girl together?" the prosecutor would ask her.

"No," she would reply.

In 1926, when he was 21, Toy moved to Dallas. He studied accounting at a business college, then got a job as an auditor with Trinity Universal Insurance Co. During his first three years in Dallas, he lived with James and Georgia Godfrey, his brother-in-law and his half-sister, on Madera Street. Then he rented a place of his own.

In 1924, when she was 17, Mae finished high school and enrolled at what was then John Tarleton State College in Stephenville, where she was very popular. When she finished Tarleton — it was a junior college then — she enrolled at Texas Tech and earned a degree in psychology. In the fall of 1930, she moved to Dallas, too. She took a teaching job at Winnetka School in Oak Cliff for $40 a month and registered for graduate work at Southern Methodist University.

She hadn't seen Toy for eight years. But when she was settled, she wrote a note inviting him to call on her. He did.

Sometime that fall, Toy brought Mae to the Godfrey home and introduced her to James and Georgia, and they would get together from time to time to play bridge. About a year later, the Godfreys learned that Toy and Mae were living together, and that Toy's teen-age sister, Mina, was living with them.

Both James and Georgia would testify that they assumed Toy and Mae were married. But they apparently never asked when or where the wedding took place or why they hadn't been invited to attend. Then one day, during a conversation with Georgia, Mae revealed that she and Toy were living together out of wedlock.

Georgia was upset. She knew that if Gatewood Lafayette Woolley, the patriarch of the large Woolley clan — he had sired 10 children by two wives — were to find out that young Mina had been living in such an unrespectable domestic environment, there would be hell to pay. She urged Mae to marry Toy before that happened.

Mae wasn't interested. It was a policy of the Dallas school board at that time that female teachers must be single. If she were to marry Toy, she would lose her job. Besides, she said, Toy wasn't the first man with whom she had had an affair. And, she said, he might not be the last. She wasn't ready to marry.

Georgia enlisted her husband in a campaign to apply pressure to both Mae and Toy.

If Mae would marry Toy, the Godfreys told her, she could file for a divorce immediately. They just wanted the couple to appear to have been married during the time that Mina lived with them.

Finally, Mae acquiesced. On March 11, 1933, she and Toy drove to Hugo, Okla., and got married. It was a "courtesy affair," Mae would testify, meant only "to save his name with his family." She said Toy had promised to divorce her immediately.

On the same day — apparently only a few hours after his wedding — Toy applied to rent a room that Mrs. Joynes had advertised at her home on Elliott Street. He told her he was single. Mae moved into a room of her own on Belmont Street. But when the school term ended in June, Mae and Toy rented an apartment and moved back in together.

Their marital bliss, if they enjoyed any, didn't last. Within a week, Mae was demanding a divorce. Toy resisted, but finally said he would grant her one if he could be the one to file for it. Mae agreed, packed her bags and went home to Comanche County. Shortly, Toy drove to the Cantrell farm and begged her to return to Dallas with him. Instead, they took a trip to Galveston to talk over the possibility of making a success of their marriage.

"I decided we could never be happy," Mae said. She went back to her parents, and Toy returned to Dallas. On July 12, he filed for divorce. In his petition, he charged that soon after their wedding, Mae had begun "a course of cruel treatment, disagreed with him continuously and that he could not please her at all."

"She did not want to live with me," Toy would tell the reporters at the jail after his arrest. "She preferred the company of other men to mine."

Meanwhile, at the house on Elliott Street, Mrs. Joynes had learned that Toy was courting Dorothy. "If I had known he was married at the time, he could not have gone with my daughter except over my dead body," she would testify.

Then, on the afternoon of Aug. 26 — two days before his divorce was final — Toy, carrying a suitcase, was starting out the door with Dorothy. "Well, Mrs. Joynes," he said, "Dorothy and I are going to Oklahoma to be married."

"I told him I didn't think that a very honorable thing to do — start off like that without telling me before," Mrs. Joynes said. "I asked him to put the marriage off for a while. . . . I suggested they could have a nice home wedding later on. But he walked off with Dorothy.

". . . They returned the next day. They said they had been married. But Dorothy had no wedding ring on her finger."

The newlyweds lived with Mrs. Joynes for a week, then bought the cottage on Ellsworth. For the first two days of their marriage, Toy was a bigamist.

The prosecutor asked Mrs. Joynes: "Did you know that four days after this marriage, while he was living under your roof, accepting your hospitality and living with your daughter, that he had written his first wife and told her he had married again, but did not love the girl he married?"

"No, sir."

". . . Or that he told his first wife he soon expected to make enough money to gain her back again?"

"Oh, no!"

The prosecutor already had placed into evidence a letter that Mae had received from Toy four days after he married Dorothy. It was one of the letters that J.J. Cantrell had turned over to the police. It told of the divorce being granted, and continued:

" . . . I am married again, and am here to say I do not love her and never will. Words will not express my feeling about it, but I intend to take care of you, all the time. You are before anyone in the world to me.

" . . . Yes, it was a radical thing to do. . . . I did it, you know why and I expect to make enough money to gain you back again soon, Darling. Please stay close to me, for I love you above anything else on this earth. I want to marry you again as soon as I can and I expect to have some money, too.

" . . . Sweet, please stay with me for I am lower than I will ever be anymore in my life. . . . I need your help, as I always have. I hope and pray for you to come back every day that passes. I hope you will write me and tell me you will marry me again, if I will build myself up and make some money. Will you, Darling, *please*.

"Write me by return mail, Darling. I love you and need you every hour. Always and forever. TGW."

According to the newspapers, Dallas had never seen a trial to compare with the one that began on Monday, Dec. 4, 1933, in Criminal District Court No. 2, Judge Noland G. Williams presiding.

From the moment District Attorney Bob Hurt rose to read the indictment, through 10 days of testimony by 113 witnesses and almost five hours of final arguments, the city would be transfixed by the sad and sordid drama unfolding in the courthouse.

"The courtroom, by the time a session opens, is so packed that the spectators cannot move a hand," a *Dallas Morning News* reporter wrote. "The doors into the corridor were opened . . . but the crowd in the hall became so boisterous that Judge Williams ordered the doors closed and the hall cleared. Instead of leaving, the overflow crowd went into the courtroom across the hall and sat chatting about the trial. . . . Some of the spectators who arrived before 8 o'clock in the morning did not leave their seats until the night session closed. . . . Persons who were forced to leave the courtroom because they had to go and prepare dinner for hubby or go feed the baby, sold their seats. Two front row seats were reported to have sold for $1 each."

They brought lunches in brown bags and threw their bread crusts and fruit rinds on the floor. They paid tips to people who brought them water and soft drinks. Souvenir hunters stole buttons off the coats of the court bailiffs.

Five women fainted. Several were hurt in the press of the crowd against doors, windows and walls. Dr. Horace Duncan, the county health officer, was called upon twice to give medical aid to persons overcome. A man who suffered a heart attack groaned so loudly as he was being carried from the courtroom that Judge Williams sent the jury upstairs until the commotion had ended.

Through it all, the papers said,"Woolley sat as if he had no great concern with the case, remaining calm throughout the day while attorneys repeatedly referred to the tragic death only a month ago of his young wife. He wore a navy blue suit, light blue shirt and darker blue tie. His shoes were freshly polished, and his blond hair parted in the middle. At one time in the proceedings . . . Woolley smiled, and his eyes sparkled with good humor."

Aligned behind the defendant, in the front row of the audience, were three of Toy's brothers, the Godfreys, and Gatewood Lafayette Woolley, the 59-year-old patriarch. "Woolley's father . . . a heavy man in comparison with his slender son, sat stolidly throughout the day," a reporter wrote. "He wore dark trousers, upheld by suspenders, a blue shirt with white stripes, a collar open and no tie. In his shirt pocket was a cigar case."

Also among the spectators was Otto Schubert, manager of the Adolphus Hotel, and his lawyer, Martin Winfrey, who told reporters: "Mr. Schubert is thinking about staging an affair like this in the junior ballroom of the Adolphus. Ought to go over big at a two-bits gate, shouldn't it?"

Indeed, the case provided all that an entertainment-hungry public could desire: a bloody killing; a young, beautiful victim; a young, passionate slayer; a *femme fatale*; sex; money; a touch of bigamy; a prosecutor demanding the electric chair. And almost as fascinating as the case itself and the tangled life of its defendant were the lawyers who were arguing it.

On the side of the state were arrayed District Attorney Hurt, his assistant, Dean Gauldin, and Ted Monroe, a special prosecutor. He had been hired by Esta and Ralph Joynes, who now were convinced that Toy had murdered Dorothy. Mr. Monroe had made a reputation for himself as a defender of persons charged with murder. His presence at the side of the D.A. was "an incongruous but colorful factor in the prosecution," the papers said.

Sitting alone beside his client at the defense table was Currie McCutcheon, a former county prosecutor who also was recognized as one of the best lawyers in the state. However, he had been in semi-retirement because of ill health, and hadn't appeared in a criminal trial in 10 years. "He wore the inevitable white carnation in his buttonhole, questioned jurors in his slightly nasal, but not unpleasant voice, and fingered an automatic pencil," a reporter wrote. Mr. McCutcheon characterized his client as "indiscreet, but not guilty of murder."

"The state says that this young man, Toy G. Woolley, willfully, maliciously and voluntarily murdered his little wife, a beautiful young woman," he told each potential juror. "Toy, here, says it was an accident. Would you require that the state prove beyond a reasonable doubt that it was intentional?"

From the beginning, Mr. McCutcheon's plan for Toy's defense puzzled the prosecutors. Indeed, he didn't seem to have a plan. He asked for no postponements, tried no delaying tactics. Instead, he demanded that Toy be tried as speedily as possible. During jury selection, the prosecutors freely exercised their right to reject potential jurors they didn't want, but Mr. McCutcheon rejected no one. He accepted men who admitted they already had formed opinions about the case. He even approved the seating of M.J. Carroll, who said Dorothy had once worked for him.

In only three hours, the jury had been seated. It was said to be a Dallas County record in a capital case.

And throughout the trial, Mr. McCutcheon allowed the prosecutors to treat the witnesses however they wished and ask them anything they wanted, rarely rising to offer an objection. At one point, a frustrated Mr. Monroe got upset that Mr. McCutcheon wasn't objecting enough. He demanded that the judge "make this defendant's lawyer come out in the open and fight." He complained that Mr. McCutcheon's handling of the case "placed the state in an embarrassing position" when prosecutors had to register objections of their own.

Mr. McCutcheon replied that he simply was eager for the jury to hear all the facts, and that his defense would come in due time, when Toy himself would take the stand.

The state's star witness, Mae Cantrell, testified on the second day. Wearing a brown wool belted suit with a green knit yoke and collar, a brown felt hat banded with ribbon, kid gloves, and gold-rimmed spectacles, she was a picture of the prim schoolteacher.

Under Mr. Monroe's careful guidance, she told of her unconventional relationship with Toy, their marriage and divorce, and his obsessive efforts to win her back. In the letter in which Toy had begged her to marry him again, he also offered to pay her expenses if she would come to Dallas and talk things over with him. On Saturday, Aug. 30, the day after she received the letter and only four days after Toy's marriage to Dorothy, she arrived by bus and registered at the Jefferson Hotel.

Toy came to her room. Mae told him she had been fired from her teaching job because of their marriage, even though their divorce was in progress when school officials found her out. She was about to transfer to the University of Texas in Austin, she said. She wanted to know whether Toy would continue helping with her school expenses, as he had done when she was at SMU. Toy told her he would.

On Sunday, they took a drive around the city, and on Monday Toy drove her home to Comanche County. Toy continued to write and phone her, she said, begging her to come back to him. Late in September, she said, he went to Austin and declared: "If Dorothy won't give me a divorce, I'll get rid of her some other way."

"Throughout the long period of questioning . . . the defendant Woolley looked at her intently," the *Morning News* reported. "At infrequent intervals, she glanced in his direction, but averted her eyes the greater part of the time. Her answers were given in a soft voice, and frequently she paused before answering a question, frowning as if to make sure of dates, hours or places before making a statement."

At 6 a.m. on Saturday, Nov. 4 — the day he was supposed to be hunting ducks in East Texas — Toy called Mae and said he was on his way to Austin. When he arrived, he picked her up at her rooming house and took her to his room at the Stephen F. Austin Hotel.

"We stayed from 8:45 until 10:15 a.m.," she testified. "He refused to let me leave and locked the door and put a chair in front of it. He said there was going to be a showdown, that I was going to promise to marry him again or do something about the money I owed him.

"I told him I owed him no money. He apparently wished me to submit to his desires then, and I refused. He said I would not leave the room alive, and that he would not leave alive.

"I became afraid and insisted I had to be at an 11 o'clock class. He took me to the campus in his car, and when I got out I told him I never was going to see him again. He wanted to know about the money again. I walked off, and when I was halfway across the campus he caught me and forced me to go back to the car. He probably would have forced me to go into the car if some students had not come up, and he then let me go."

Mae went into the administration building and phoned her new fiance, E.W. Shuey, described in the newspapers as "a traveling man of Austin." He picked her up and drove her home.

"About 4 o'clock that afternoon, Toy called me and implied he was going to kill himself," Mae testified. "He asked me to attend to his affairs in Dallas. I told him I would."

Then about 9:30 that Saturday night, Toy called Mae from Dallas. "He was excited," she said. "He told me that Dorothy had been in a serious accident and was not expected to live. . . . He told me that if I would not marry Mr. Shuey, he would give me $1,000 before the end of the week. Mr. Shuey was with me at the time and listened over the telephone. I read of the shooting of Dorothy in the noon papers Monday."

Mae said Toy also had threatened suicide about a week before he married Dorothy. He turned on the gas in the room where they were talking, she said. She turned it off. Then he tried unsuccessfully to choke himself.

Mr. McCutcheon, cross-examining her, asked: "Did you ever love him?"

"I hardly know how to answer that," Mae said.

"Well, did you?"

Mae looked down at her hands and said: "What is the test of love?"

On Nov. 6, the day of Dorothy's funeral, Mae withdrew from the University of Texas. Her registration card, which listed Toy as her "guardian," said her reason was "lack of finances."

After she had finished testifying, Mae granted an interview. "He never did love me," she told the reporter. "He didn't say the things other men would, nor act as they would."

The reporter said, "But you must have had a terrible fascination for him, an overpowering charm, if he did what the state claims."

"I don't know. I don't understand. It all puzzles me."

Mae said she sensed that many of the people in the courtroom, "the women, particularly," were bitter toward her. "But I had to do it. I was afraid. It was either tell this story, much as I hated it, or run the risk of being killed myself."

Many of the hostile people were from Comanche County. Mae said she knew of only two families in Lamkin who hadn't come the 125 miles to Dallas for the trial. "You know how a little town is," she said. "They're just eating it up, talking and talking, as little towns do. . . .

"And Toy, he stands out in the corridor there during the recesses and stares and stares at me. I guess he hates me. If looks could kill . . . ."

Mr. McCutcheon began his defense by calling 88 character witnesses — from Comanche and Hamilton counties, from Ellsworth Avenue and from Trinity Universal Insurance Co. — to testify that Toy was an honest, truth-telling man and had the respect of the people who knew him. Several of the Lamkin people testified that Mae didn't enjoy such a sterling reputation among her neighbors.

Then on Thursday, Mr. McCutcheon announced to the reporters that Toy would take the stand in his own defense, probably Thursday night or Friday morning.

"What the defendant will say about how his young wife met her untimely death is the principal thing the jury and followers of the trial want to know," the *Times Herald* reported. " . . . In fact, the entire defense, while hard to analyze and understand in all details, has been mostly a 'build-up' for the defendant's own story of the shooting.

"His burden, though, has been made heavy by the state in the criss-cross of circumstances pointing to a murder motive. Woolley, the state claims, may find it easy to tell how Dorothy was killed, but not so easy to explain many of his actions, and the telephone calls and letters he wrote to Miss Cantrell during the time he was married to Dorothy."

But the week ended without Toy coming to the stand. A bailiff took the jury to a movie at the Majestic Theater Saturday night, services at City Temple Church Sunday morning, and a bus ride around the city Sunday afternoon. Court reporter Jack Tingle said he had taken down 300,000 words of testimony in shorthand, and estimated he would pass the 500,000-word mark before the end of the trial. The *Morning News* said this was about the same length as Victor Hugo's *Les Miserables*.

Monday night, Mr. McCutcheon put Mina on the stand and asked the judge's permission to set up Toy and Dorothy's bedroom furniture in the courtroom.

"The courtroom was packed until there was no breathing space," the *Times Herald* reported. "Men and women strained to see and hear. An atmosphere of morbid expectancy hung over the room as bailiffs set up the deathbed and brought in the chair and other furniture as Mina said it was the morning of Dorothy's death."

The newspapers described Mina as "a slender, attractive young girl." She wore a red-and-black silk dress and a black, tight-fitting hat. She said she had been visiting Toy and Dorothy and had stayed with them Friday and Saturday nights.

Mr. McCutcheon showed her a picture of Dorothy and asked if that was her brother's wife. She said it was. He set the picture on the defense table in front of Toy. The jury, the judge, the spectators watched for a reaction. The state's attorneys sat silent.

"For fully five minutes, the young defendant's eyes were glued to the girl the state claims he murdered," a reporter wrote. "His lips drew tight. It appeared he was on the verge of throwing himself on the table and bursting into tears. Everyone seemed to expect him to do that. He didn't. Instead he just looked and looked."

Mr. McCutcheon then asked Mina to recreate the death scene. She sat on the vanity bench and held the shotgun as her brother had held it. She then moved to the rocker, to show the jury where she was when the gun went off. The position she took placed her directly in the line of fire. Mr. McCutcheon pointed out that if Dorothy had moved, Toy would have killed his own sister. Mina then lay across the bed in the position she said Dorothy was in.

"Now demonstrate to the jury just what happened when the gun went off," Mr. McCutcheon directed.

Mina returned to the vanity bench, held the shotgun as Toy had held it, then jumped up, dropped the gun, and sent the bench scooting across the floor.

After Mina left the stand, Mr. McCutcheon asked the district attorney to give him a copy of the statement that Toy had made after his indictment was handed down, which contained his own version of Dorothy's death. The prosecutors hadn't introduced it into evidence.

Mr. Hurt objected: "Your honor, this defendant signed this voluntary statement, and he is not entitled to it. If Mr. McCutcheon wants to know how this shooting happened, he can ask his client about it."

Mr. McCutcheon replied: ". . . There is just one way I know to make the district attorney produce the voluntary statement: The defendant rests."

The reporters raced for the phones. Toy wouldn't testify after all. The prosecutors would never have a chance to question him.

The last witness, in rebuttal, was Ralph Joynes. "Gentlemen," he told the jury, "I am fully convinced that Toy Woolley deliberately killed my sister. I want you to know that I hate him with all my heart."

Mr. Monroe's closing argument was an hour and 40 minutes long. Mr. McCutcheon's was three hours long. Mr. Hurt's was an hour. He demanded the death penalty. The jury got the case at 1:32 a.m. Wednesday. It returned to the courtroom at 9:45 a.m.

Judge Williams read the verdict: "We, the jury, find the defendant not guilty."

Immediately, the courtroom was in an uproar. Mr. McCutcheon shouted: "Your honor, may truth always prevail in your court!" Gatewood Lafayette Woolley threw his arms around Toy's neck and cried: "Thank God, I'll get my boy back!" Sisters and brothers scrambled over the railing and smothered Toy with embraces and kisses.

Jurors told reporters they had taken only three votes. The first two had been 10-to-2 for acquittal. The third had been unanimous. They were convinced by Mina's testimony, they said, and were suspicious of the prosecution for not introducing Toy's statement into evidence and not allowing Mr. McCutcheon to see it. The state had left reasonable doubts in their minds.

Sheriff's deputies hustled Toy back to the jail, where he had lived for 31 days. As he was being released from custody, Mr. McCutcheon told him, "Get your things and go home to your mother. Never go back to the cottage where you and Dorothy lived. Never take anything that is associated with it. Try to forget."

Toy gave Dorothy's .22 rifle to Deputy Fred Bradberry, who had guarded him during the trial. He gave his shotgun to Deputy Ted Hinton, who had maintained order in the courtroom.

"You've treated me fine," Toy said to them.

He posed for newspaper photographers, then got into a taxi with his father and sped away.

So I still don't know whether Uncle Toy murdered his wife. Maybe nobody ever knew, except him. Maybe not even he knew for sure. I know he married at least twice more. I heard that he was a good son and took care of his mother — my grandmother — in her old age. I heard he was in his 70s when he died, and that he was a court bailiff in Lubbock at the time. I heard that Aunt Mina died at an early age, of natural causes. I have no idea what ever happened to Mae.

But there's another, last story about the gun.

Not long ago, a friend mentioned an old newspaper page to me. It was framed and hanging on a wall of the Bonnie and Clyde Suite — Room 305 — of the Stockyards Hotel in Fort Worth, he said. Bonnie Parker and Clyde Barrow hid out from the law in that room for a time, so its walls are covered now with pictures of them. One of Bonnie's guns is in a glass box, and there are newspaper clippings about the Louisiana ambush that six officers set for Bonnie and Clyde on May 23, 1934, about five months after Uncle Toy's trial.

I drove to Fort Worth and read the old page, published the day after the ambush. Spread across it is a story that Bob Alcorn and Ted Hinton, Dallas County deputy sheriffs, told a reporter from the *Dallas Dispatch*. They're describing how they and the others killed Bonnie and Clyde.

"You couldn't hear any one shot," Deputy Alcorn is saying. "It was just a roar, a continuous roar, and it kept up for several minutes. We emptied our guns, reloaded and kept shooting. . . .

"As we jumped into sight, I could see Clyde reaching as if to get his gun, but he never had a chance to fire a shot. Neither did Bonnie, though we learned a few minutes later that they both were carrying rifles across their laps.

"Each of us six officers had a shotgun and an automatic rifle and pistols. We opened fire with the automatic rifles. They were emptied before the car got even with us. Then we used shotguns.

"Ted's was the shotgun given him by Toy Woolley after his trial in Dallas for the death of his wife. It was the gun Woolley was cleaning when the thing went off and killed the girl. . . ."

May 1992

THE HANDS AND EYE OF TEXAS BILLY MAYS

In July of 1990 I was on a plane from Dallas to Denver and fell into conversation with my seatmate. He had the look of an aging cowboy - boots, jeans, Budweiser jacket, gray hair, thick spectacles. He asked me my trade, and I told him I was a journalist, on my way to South Dakota to do a story about the Sioux. He told me that he played shuffleboard for a living and was on his way to a tournament in Nebraska. I said, "You know, way back in the '60s I read a story in Sports Illustrated about a shuffleboard hustler named Texas Billy Mays. I wonder whatever happened to him." And my seatmate replied, "I'm Billy Mays." This story, which I wrote several months later, was reprinted in The Best American Sports Writing: 1991.

IT COULD EASILY HAVE TURNED OUT WRONG, TEXAS BILLY MAYS IS saying. If he hadn't fallen off that oil derrick on that day so long ago, if he hadn't been dating that waitress, if Granville Humphrey hadn't come into Sam's Bar, there's no telling whichaway his life might have gone.

"The way I see it," he says, "every man is born with the ability to do something better than anybody else can do that thing. The trouble is, most men never find out what their thing is. I'm one of the lucky ones. I found the one thing I can do better than anybody."

Billy's sitting at a table in Click's, a bar and game room on Northwest Highway in Dallas, drinking a beer, explaining.

It was 1958, he says. He was 21 and not long off the family farm up at Emory, near Sulphur Springs. The derrick was on a rig in the Gulf of Mexico, off Louisiana. Billy's fall broke his back. While he healed, he hung out at Sam's Bar on Haskell Avenue in Dallas, where his girlfriend worked. "They had a shuffleboard in there," Billy says, "but I didn't pay any attention to it. Hell, I didn't even know what a shuffleboard was."

Then one day, Granville Humphrey walked in. "He came from Oklahoma City," Billy says. "He had beat everybody in Dallas. He was the world's champion."

The bar patrons started drawing partners for a shuffleboard round robin. Thirty-nine players signed up. They needed a 40th. They talked Billy into giving it a try.

"It turned out, me and Granville Humphrey drew partners," Billy says. "He toted me, I guess you'd say. We won the round robin. I played the rest of the day and lost the $40 I'd won, but I'd been hooked. I'd be at Sam's when they opened up in the morning, and I wouldn't leave till they shut the door at midnight. At the end of three months, I was the best shuffleboard player in Dallas. By the time I was 22, I was the best in the world."

In the kind of shuffleboard played by passengers on cruise ships and senior citizens in St. Petersburg, they shove pucks about the deck or floor with long sticks. That isn't the kind that Billy Mays learned at Sam's Bar.

Billy's is the *true* shuffleboard, the *original* shuffleboard, the shuffleboard played in English taverns as early at 1532 and by the early settlers as soon as they had been on the shore of North America long enough to build taverns of their own.

The modern version of the game is played on a slab of rock maple that's 20 feet, 8 inches long. The slab sits on a table and is surrounded by a padded trough. The players stand at one end of the table and, taking turns, slide four metal weights each toward the other end. The board has been sprinkled with powdered wax to make the weights slide quickly and smoothly. The player who places a weight closest to the opposite end of the board without its dropping off scores points. Then the weights are shot from the other end of the table. In the most commonly played variety of the game, the first player — or, in the case of doubles, the first team — to score 15 points is the winner.

Every beer joint worthy of the name has its shuffleboard, along with its pool table and its jukebox loaded with country music, and Billy knows where they all are.

"Just in the state of Texas, I'd say there's 5,000 boards now," he says. "California's got probably 6,000. Washington and Oregon together has got more than California has. They play a lot in Connecticut and Maine and Massachusetts, but there's no good players up there. There's a couple of good players in New York. Pennsylvania's got the best on the East Coast. Michigan, Indiana and Illinois have a lot of boards, but there's just five or six places in Iowa to play it. Nebraska's real full of them. Kansas has got quite a few, and Colorado. There's 50 or 100 in Montana, but just a few in Wyoming. North Dakota's got a couple. South Dakota's got, I'd say, 20. Idaho don't have very many. . . . "

Shuffleboard is a favorite pastime of cowboys, truck drivers, farmers, miners, construction workers, people who work hard with their hands, but a lot of businessmen and city-slicker professionals play it, too. Shuffleboard players like to bet on their games, and they listen to loud music, drink beer and smoke cigarettes while they play. Maybe that's why the game looks so much easier than it is. Nobody seems to be straining at it.

"But it's the toughest game in the world," Billy says. "It's a combination of Bobby Fischer type chess, Arnold Palmer type golf and Muhammad Ali type nerve. There's very little luck in it and a tremendous amount of skill. It's a precision game."

Looking at Billy, you would never peg him for the world's greatest master of the world's toughest game. He's so wiry he could be mistaken for scrawny. He dresses in cowboy boots and satin jackets that advertise beer. His glasses are so thick that his eyes seem outlandishly large. Maybe because of the glasses, his brow is always furrowed horizontally, giving him an air of perpetual bemusement, as if he doesn't know quite where he is, or as if he's trying to find a familiar face in a crowd.

One of the thick lenses isn't very useful. When Billy was 9 years old, a rock from his brother's slingshot struck him in the right eye, robbing it of sight. He can distinguish light and dark with it, he says, but nothing else. Then, when he was 17, he fought a boxing match in Longview against Donnie Fleeman — who later would KO Ezzard Charles — and was knocked cross-eyed by a blow to the back of his head. "When I get tired, that right eye still wanders a little," Billy says. "I can't hold the thing still."

But it doesn't matter much. "I don't look at the weights when I shoot anyway," he says. "I shoot with my mind. If you turn the weight loose right at your end of the table, it'll go right at the other end. What you've got to do is read the drift, and then you shoot into the drift."

Every shuffleboard is as unique as a fingerprint. Its humps and warps and quirks and curves, its slow spots and fast spots — all undetectable to the eye — make up a board's drift, and the drift is what gives it its character. "The drift is part of the table," Billy says, "but the drift isn't always the same. Weather can change it. Putting a matchbook under one of the table legs can change it.

"When you go play someone on their own table," he says, "it's a bigger advantage to them than when you play a football team on its home field. A guy who plays on a board all the time, he'll know every little drift in it. It's like spotting him three or four points. But in about two games, I'll know the board better than him. I watch. I study what the board does. It's like opening a book and studying it instead of just opening a book and reading."

Billy finishes his beer and walks over to the shuffleboard. It's a board he knows well, for it's a World's Best, his own brand, built by Texas Billy Mays himself at his shop in Seagoville. His signature is on it.

It's what he does for most of his living these days, he says, building and selling shuffleboards for $3,200 to $4,500 each and packaging and selling cans of his special shuffleboard wax, which he says is "the fastest wax on the market," mixed according to his own secret formula. But tonight Click's is paying him $500 to perform trick shots for the customers and then play all challengers.

He starts simple. His wife, Doris, sets two weights on the table at the other end. Billy slides two weights down and knocks them off simultaneously. He repeats the trick using three weights. Then Doris sets two weights on the table and lays a cigarette across them like a rail. Billy slides a weight between them and knocks the cigarette away without touching the two weights supporting it. Then Doris sets a weight near the end of the table and stands a penny against it, on edge. Billy's shot knocks the penny away without touching the weight. Then his grand finale: Billy blindfolds himself with bar napkins, shoves two weights down the board simultaneously and knocks off two weights at the corners of the other end.

Then for three hours he plays 11-point games against all comers. He's handicapped by a finger he broke two weeks earlier when he dropped a shuffleboard on it, but he still beats them all. At Click's and other bars where Billy has put on his exhibition over the years, he has played more than 300 games and has lost only one. "They don't pay me for losing," he says.

But $500 is a far cry from the sums his barroom game used to earn him. In 1962, for instance, when he beat Bob Miles out of $22,000 at the Park Inn Diner in Buena Vista, Calif. That was the match that notified the shuffleboard world that Texas Billy Mays was a force to be feared. Five years later, Billy told *Sports Illustrated* about it:

"We played for 30 hours," Billy says. "'Let's play for $100,' Bob Miles said. 'Let's play for $200,' I said. 'Make it $300,' he said. 'Make it $400,' I said. There were 120 people in there betting, and only three were betting on me. I won 18 in a row — 19 out of 21. He went busted five times and had to go get money. While he was gone, I played $500 freeze-out with Mexican Tommy — he's an interior decorator who has the most beautiful shot in shuffleboard, it's poetry in motion — and K.C. Chuck. K.C. started betting on me after I busted *him*. Won $4,800. Another boy won $4,000. Some nights you throw those weights up there, looks like someone stops them with a string."

For 25 years after he fell off the oil derrick, Billy never worked at what most people would call a regular job. Sometimes he would sell and repair shuffleboards for the National Shuffleboard Co. From time to time he would come back to Dallas and toil awhile as a carpenter. But most of the time he was on the road, playing shuffleboard in glitzy big-city lounges and fly-blown roadside honky-tonks from Philadelphia to Los Angeles and Detroit to Houston for whatever money the locals were willing to bet on their hometown heroes.

He once bet $1,000 a game in Pasco, Wash., and walked out with $10,000. He once won $10,000 in Stockton, Calif., too, "but that was mostly hot checks," he says.

In the Gay '90s Bar in Hollywood, he played Rock Hudson for $100 a game. "I beat him three games in a row," Billy says. "Then, as I usually did, I tried to jack up the stakes. I said, 'Well, let's play for $200 a game now,' and Rock Hudson said, 'Naw, $100.' And I said, 'Well, if you won't play for $200, I quit.' I was trying to bluff him, see. But he said, 'Damn, I'm sure glad you quit, because I'd hate to have to stay here until I won a game.'"

The best pickings, though, were in the small towns of the West and Midwest, those with 500 souls, or 1,000, one of whom regularly beat everybody at the local beer joint and thought of himself as God's gift to shuffleboard.

"In those little places, I could always get a game," Billy says, "because the town people would force their local hotshot to play me. They would say, 'Aw, come on, Jimmy,' or whatever the guy's name was, 'I got a $100 bill that says you can beat him.' The longer we play, the more determined the guy is to beat me, and pretty soon I've really got a hustle going."

In the popular mind, a hustler always allows his opponent to win a few games to set him up for the kill, then raises the stakes and destroys him. But Billy never did it that way.

"I always went in and beat them as bad as I could right off the bat," he says. "That makes them want to play more. See, if you play somebody and let them win, they've got your money in their pocket, and they can quit. A lot of times, that's the reason they'll play you, thinking you're a hustler and you're going to let them win a few. But I just went in and beat them as bad as I could, and then I'd laugh at them a little bit. If you laugh at a man, he's going to want to play you again. His pride makes him do it."

As Billy's reputation grew, he sometimes had to resort to deception to lure someone into a game. "One time I was coming from Canada into Denver," he says, "and I didn't think I would get much action there because I had beat them a couple of months before out of a couple of thousand. So I stopped at a drugstore and bought an Ace bandage and wrapped my right hand in it and put my arm in a sling. Boy, they just jumped on me, and I beat them out of about $1,200. So the next day, I wrapped my left hand, just to see if anybody would notice. Not a soul noticed that I had changed hands."

Robbie Gann of Visalia, Calif., remembers him in those days. "He used to come through the door bragging that he was the greatest shuffleboard player that ever lived," she says. "And if they didn't want to play him, he would say, 'Well, I'll play you one-handed.' And if they said no, then he would say, 'Well, I'll tie one hand behind me and wear a blindfold.'"

"He was the undisputed champion for like 15 years," says Robbie's sister-in-law, Charlene Goldsmith. "He would step up to the board, and he would play anybody. He never told nobody he wouldn't play them. My husband said the classiest thing about Billy that's ever been said. He said, 'Billy's talent is surpassed only by his ego.' And after he won, sometimes he would have to fight his way out of a bar, he made everybody so mad."

"I've always been a good loser," Billy says, "but I'm a bad winner. I like to rub their nose in it."

Charlene and her husband, California Bob Goldsmith, own Mr. G's in Visalia. In 1967, their bar was sponsoring a shuffleboard team in a Sacramento tournament, and they went to watch.

"I had heard and heard about Billy Mays this and Billy Mays that — world champion, you know — and I was really looking forward to meeting Texas Billy Mays," Charlene says. "But when we got to Sacramento, somebody told us Billy was in the hospital having stomach surgery. He had ulcers, I think. Well, all of a sudden everybody's twittering, you know, saying, 'There's Billy Mays!' and he walks in the door, and he's all bent over. Bent almost double. The doctor wouldn't release him out of the hospital, but he had left anyway. And he walks over to a board and starts playing a game for $100 an in. Back in 1967, $100 an in was pretty good money."

Billy remembers that tournament. "I won the triple crown," he says. "I won the singles, I won the doubles, and I won the team event."

He burned up 100,000 miles of highway and three or four used cars a year in those days, getting from bar to bar and tournament to tournament, and sometimes circumstances forced him to depend on the kindness of friends.

"Billy used to come to our house and spend the night," Charlene says. "We never knew who he was going to show up with. One time it was a Canadian. One time it was an Indian. You just never knew with him. It was always 'Hello, Billy, and who is *she*?' He traveled like a Gypsy all the time, him and whatever wife or woman he was with. A shuffleboard player can resist anything except temptation."

Billy acknowledges that his marital record is smudged. He has had seven wives, four of them before he was 21. "My first wife was Sue," he says, "my second wife was Sybil, my third was Sandra, my fourth wife was Jean, my fifth wife was Myrna. . . . Naw, my fifth wife was Sheila, my sixth wife was Myrna and my seventh is Doris. Me and all my wives but one get along real good."

Billy and Doris have been married five years. Jean lasted fifteen years, Sybil only 90 days. "Sybil was one of them whirlwinds," Billy says. "That was back when I was drinking a little bit, and a bunch of us got drunk, and the next thing I know I was married."

"Sometimes," Charlene says, "Billy would call and say, 'Bobby, can you send me a couple of hundred? I've had a bad run of luck.' And it wasn't that he had shot bad and lost, it was just that things had happened, you know. So Bobby would send him the money. And the very next time we would see him, Billy would come up and pay Bobby that money back. We never failed to send it to him because he always paid it back.

"One time when he was at our house, our little boy wanted to play him. He wanted to play the world champ. So Billy played him. You think he would let that kid win? You know what Billy said to him when they got through? He said, 'You'd better work on your left, kid.' Billy never *let* anybody win anything."

About seven years ago, Billy gave up the road and came home to Dallas and settled down. "It got to where nobody would play me," he says. "It got to where I couldn't make a living no more."

Billy often calls himself "the world champion shuffleboard player." Other players call him that, too. Still others say he used to be the world champion but isn't anymore. Asked who has replaced him as world champion, some just shrug. Others name another player, but no two are likely to name the same player.

How a player becomes "world champion" isn't clear. Billy used to promote a competition in Las Vegas called the World Championship Shuffleboard Tournament. He won it the last time it was played, in 1984, so maybe he's the reigning champion until another tournament with that name is played.

If the title is based on the number of tournaments won over the years, few would question Billy's right to it. "I haven't kept a count of them," he says. "I'd say I've won seven or eight hundred. Back when I played all the time, I won about 75 out of 100."

Or maybe Billy's personal way of determining who has the right to the title is the best. It's certainly the simplest. "If you beat everybody," he says, "you're the world champion."

He still plays some friendly round robins in bars around Dallas, and every now and then he'll enter a tournament in Houston or Austin or Fort Worth, somewhere close at hand, but he admits he's getting rusty. And then there's that broken finger, still bothering him.

But he entered January's Pacific Coast Shuffleboard Association's Shuffleboard Extravaganza II in Las Vegas just to prove that he isn't as far over the hill as rumor is beginning to say.

"You need to play a competitive game every week or two to stay in top form," he says, "and I haven't done that. It's kind of like dancing. You dance a lot, and you keep a real smooth rhythm. But if you don't dance much, you lose that step. I don't have any idea how I'll do in Las Vegas, but I want to give it a try."

He mails in his entry fees — $400 for singles and $200 for doubles competition — but the PCSA notifies him that they weren't received by deadline. His name will be added to a list of alternates who might get a chance to play if some of the entrants don't show up.

Billy is fit to be tied. "Thirty of the best players in the world are going to be there," he says. "It's the biggest tournament there is. There won't be two people in it who aren't capable of winning. But it looks like they don't want to play me."

Nevertheless, a week before the tournament is to begin, he and two friends start toward Las Vegas by car. In Big Spring, they stop to play a little shuffleboard. They win $100. They stop again in Odessa and win $200, and again in Phoenix and come away with $500, more than enough to pay their road expenses. "And the whole town would come out to see us," Billy says.

Billy's room at the Showboat Hotel is free. So are his meals. The PCSA informs him that he won't be allowed to play in the singles competition, but Freddy Thuman of Auburn, Calif., who has known Billy for years, invites him to partner with him in the doubles.

The Showboat Sports Pavilion, where the tournament is to be played, is a warehouse-size room just upstairs from the bowling alleys, where the Professional Bowlers Association also is playing a tournament. The room has been fitted out with a dozen ordinary barroom shuffleboards — so ordinary that quarters have to be fed into them to activate their scoreboards.

The atmosphere of the pavilion is more akin to a saloon than a sports arena. At tables and in seats about the shuffleboards, players from all over the United States and Canada swap tales about past tournaments, difficult boards they've played, taverns where they spent memorable nights. A blue haze of cigarette smoke lies over the room like smog. Loud music blares. Bars at each end of the room do a steady business.

It's a double-elimination tournament. No one is out until he has lost two matches. A match is two out of three games. Before tournament play begins, the players are sold to "sponsors" in a Calcutta auction, which is similar to an ordinary sports pool except that the players are sold to the highest bidder. At the end of the tournament, the "owners" of the winning players are paid the contents of the Calcutta pot.

One doubles team — Darrol Nelson of Springfield, Ore., and Jim Allis of Seattle — are sold for $2,800. Billy and Freddy go for $400.

"Darrol and Jimmy are probably the best doubles team in the world right now," Billy says.

But he and Freddy get off to a fast start. Halfway into the first game, Billy has memorized the board and starts placing his weights with the precision of a diamond cutter, moving about his end of the board with an easy grace, like a dancer in slow motion. From time to time, he meets Freddy at mid-table to discuss strategy. Billy always does the talking. Freddy listens and nods.

When he isn't shooting, Billy pays no attention to the game. He walks about the crowd, waving, shaking hands, smoking, exchanging stories with old friends and foes until it's his turn to shoot again.

Freddy, on the other hand, is a wad of nerves wrapped in a bundle of emotion. Every shot to him is exquisite pain or ecstasy. He rants, groans, paces, punches at the air with his fists.

They win the match easily in two games. While most matches in the tournament are requiring two to three hours to complete, Billy and Freddy are finished in an hour and 20 minutes. That afternoon, they win their second match as easily.

The day's third match — the quarter-final round — isn't so easy. Chuck Nooris of Portland, Ore., and A.Z. Turnbolt of San Jose, Calif., win the first game, 15-8.

Freddy's face flushes. He moans, he rails. The second game becomes a tedious war of attrition. Two hours and 15 minutes after it began, Billy and Freddy win, 15-13, then win the third one quickly, 15-8, at 12:30 a.m.

Freddy dashes to the wall where the brackets are posted, to see who their opponents will be in the semifinal round. Billy doesn't bother. "You have to beat them all to win," he says. "It don't matter to me what order they come in."

The semifinal round is to begin at 8 a.m. the next day. At 7:30, Billy breakfasts on M&Ms and jogs around an island of cars in the parking lot with Freddy. Then they go inside and demolish their opponents in an hour.

Their next match — the final match of the winners' bracket — is to begin at 6 p.m., against Darrol Nelson and Jim Allis, the $2,800 Calcutta auction babies. To kill the daylight hours, Billy wanders downstairs to the card room for a game of poker.

Darrol and Jim are as good as Billy said. They begin the match with a 6-0 lead. They're very serious, very calm. They play the board like they own it. They win, 15-6.

Billy and Freddy manage to win the second, 15-14, but their shooting is erratic, and Freddy is a basket case, screaming and shaking his fists in the air. They lose the final game, 15-3.

They've clinched third place. But to win the championship, they now must beat the winners of the losers' bracket, then beat Darrol and Jim in two matches. They must do it all right now.

"They're saying you're over the hill," someone says to Billy. "Are you?"

"I tell you how you can find out," Billy replies. "Go find somebody that'll play me a game for $500."

The best of the losers — Glen Davidson of Oklahoma City and Sparky Sparkman of San Diego — demolish them, 15-2, in their first game. But Billy and Freddy win two, 15-10 and 15-14.

They've clinched second place. Their two matches against Darrol and Jim are the only matches in the tournament still to be played. A couple of dozen spectators — all that's left of the crowd — are gathered at one table now.

Billy and Freddy win the first game, 15-13.

"I've been trying to explain Billy Mays to my friend here," says a man sitting directly behind Billy, "but I can't. There's no way to explain a Billy Mays. He's the kind of guy you love to hate. He's nothing but a hustler, but if there was a shuffleboard hall of fame, he'd be the first one in it."

Billy and Freddy win the second game — and the match — 15-12.

"I'll guarantee we'll win the next match," Billy mutters to a friend. "Jim's getting drunk and Darrol's struggling."

Billy and Freddy win the first game, 15-11, and rack up a 4-1 lead in the second.

"Put them out of their misery, Billy!" Freddy shouts.

"Billy Mays has returned!" yells someone in the crowd.

But Darrol and Jim recover and win, 15-14.

At 1:25 a.m. the last game of the tournament begins. The players have been on their feet for almost eight hours without a break. The crowd has dwindled to the hard core, and most of them are drunk.

But Billy seems as fresh as if he were beginning. His movements are silken. His words to Freddy are calming. His shots are sharp and exact.

Finally, at 2:04 a.m., Freddy scores a three-point shot and wins the game, 15-10. He falls to the floor and kicks the air like a dying rabbit.

Billy and Freddy split the $3,105 first-place doubles prize money. Freddy wraps Billy in a hug. "I love you, you old son of a bitch," he says. They shake hands and say goodbye.

Billy also had bought part of himself in the $18,000 Calcutta auction pot. His share of the winnings is $2,785. After the stack of bills is counted into his hand, he announces that this has been his last tournament. "Tournaments are getting to be too much hassle," he says. "I'm getting too old for it. Let somebody else have it."

The people laugh. "Sure, Billy, sure," somebody says.

He sleeps until noon, then begins the long drive home.

March 1990

WHERE HAVE ALL THE HORNY TOADS GONE?

One day I was visiting with my friend Robert Hart, a photo editor at the Dallas Morning News. I don't remember why, but we got to talking about horny toads, and soon realized that neither of us had seen one around Dallas in a long, long time. "I think you ought to find out why and write a story about it," Robert said. So I did.

He was sitting at the junction where one of the ant highways entered the huge ant metropolis in our back yard. He was still as a stone and could have been mistaken for one, or for a dead cactus or a lump of rotten fence post.

But his beady eyes were watching the ants move along their highway, struggling under their loads of grass seed and bits of leaf. Every now and then his tongue would flick and one of the ants would disappear into his mouth. It happened so quickly that the other ants didn't seem to notice. They didn't even know he was there.

I wondered how he chose which ants he would flick. Why would he let a dozen or more pass by unharmed and then lash down like Fate upon the next? I wondered if the ants stung him on their way down his gullet.

I wondered, then I shot him with my BB gun.

He flipped onto his back, his short legs wiggled for a moment, and he died. I picked him up. Despite the thornlike horns on his head and back, his skin was incredibly soft. Especially the white skin of his belly. It was smoother than silk, and beautiful.

I held him, examined him. Then, not knowing what else to do with a dead horny toad, I threw him down.

I'm not proud of the memory. I'm not proud to say I killed many a horny toad in my time. It was something boys did in that place in those days. And horny toads were such an ordinary part of our landscape, more common than mockingbirds or armadillos or road runners or most other creatures that we associate with the Texas landscape. They were almost as common as the ants.

We didn't always shoot them. They were easy to chase down and grab, and a number of interesting things could be done with them. You could put a horned toad in your shirt pocket and release him in the classroom during study hall. You could stroke his soft belly and induce a hypnotic state that would freeze him like a statue. We called this "putting him to sleep."

Once in a blue moon you could provoke him into squirting blood from his eyes. People don't believe horny toads do this unless they've seen it. It sounds too much like the tales that old men told little boys and little boys passed on to little girls to make them wrinkle their noses and say, "Ooooo!" We tried many times to make this happen.

Then one day we angered or scared a horny toad enough, and it did. Two streams of blood, thin as threads, shot out of his eyes. It unnerved us, for we had been told that if horny toad blood hits your own eyes, you go blind. Years later I read that this actually had happened to a few people, and that they weren't permanently blinded, but their eyes stung and were inflamed for a while.

No one knows for sure why horny toads spew blood from their eyes, but in Mexico it's one of the reasons they're regarded as sacred: When they cry, they weep tears of blood.

I kept my pet horny toads in a shoe box. Whenever I thought of it, I would capture 10 or 12 ants and release them into the box for my prisoners to eat. I didn't know that a horny toad eats about 100 ants a day. Sometimes if one of my prisoners began to look peaked, I would let him go. But it's hard to tell how a horny toad is feeling, so most of them died. I'm not proud of the memory.

But I've learned lately that my friends and I weren't the deadliest enemies that the Texas horned lizard, as it's properly called — *Phrynosoma cornutum* to the scientists — has had to cope with. I'm happy to say that horny toads still thrive in our small West Texas town, as they thrived for more than 4 million years over nearly all of Texas. I've seen them out there in the Trans-Pecos, soaking up the morning sun, still zapping travelers on the ant highways.

But when did you last see one in Dallas, or anywhere east of Interstate 35 and north of Interstate 10?

"They used to be common all around here," said Dr. John Campbell, who teaches biology at the University of Texas at Arlington. "Up until the early '80s people used to bring them in all the time for identification. But they have really just disappeared."

Ken Seleske, curator of education at the Fort Worth Zoo, used to have a colony of four or five horny toads in his backyard watermelon patch. "I had a red harvester ant bed in my yard that I babied and took care of as a food source for them," he said, "and I kept cats out of my yard. The horned lizards were there for years. Then they mysteriously went belly up and died on me."

He told me about a neighbor: "When his children were little, 25 or 30 years ago, they kept seeing horned lizards in their yard, and they wondered whether they were seeing the same ones over and over or whether there were just lots of them. One day they decided that every time they saw one they would put it in their sandbox and count them at the end of the day. They collected over 80, just in the yard, in one day. But they're gone. Today you couldn't find one in the whole neighborhood."

I called Jim Hoggard, a friend in Wichita Falls, which is west of the I-35 corridor, to see how the horny toads were doing up there. "When we moved into our house in 1976, we had horny toads in our yard," he said. "I remember trying to interest my daughter into bending down close enough to one to see it squirt blood. She wouldn't do it. She didn't believe me. But I haven't seen one around here in at least 10 years."

I called my brother in Cisco, 100 miles west of Fort Worth. Last time I walked across his pasture, about 12 years ago, horny toads scurried like cockroaches.

"Seen any horny toads lately?" I asked.

Dick's a banker. I had called him at work. There was a long silence. "No," he finally said.

Cisco, by the way, is in Eastland County, where an embalmed horny toad in a velvet-lined casket is on display in the lobby of the courthouse. Dick said he would call me next time he saw a horny toad. I haven't heard from him.

And I'm not likely to, the experts tell me. The chances of a horny toad surviving in this part of Texas these days are none. "They can't survive in parking lots," Dr. Campbell said. "They can't breed on concrete." And two other enemies harry the horny toad even more implacably than the real estate developers: the South American fire ant and the North Texas lawn lover.

"Fire ants attack and kill animals as large as a white-tail deer fawn," Mr. Seleske said. "A little horned lizard coming out of an egg is easy prey for them."

The fire ants also are wiping out the red harvester ants that are the horny toad's food supply. And if a horny toad escapes the fire ants and starvation, he's almost certain to be killed, along with the harvester ants and every other kind of bug life, by the folks who are out spraying poisonous chemicals on their Bermuda.

That's what Mr. Seleske thinks happened to the little guys who used to hang around his watermelon patch. "The people who live around me are into heavy chemical use on their lawns. The horned lizards probably got into some Amdro or something in a neighbor's yard."

So the humble Texas horned lizard, the thorny little companion and plaything of my childhood, is listed by the state as a "threatened species." I asked Andrew Price, a Texas Parks and Wildlife zoologist, what that means.

"There's worry about the future of the species in the state," he said. "It means it's against the law to kill one or to capture one and take it out of the wild. It means that, in the rare event that somebody sees a horned lizard, they should leave it alone."

As I said, I'm not proud of the memory.

July 1991

THE DEATH OF AUSTIN SQUATTY

John Jenkins was a brilliant scholar of Texas history and books about Texas history. And he was an internationally known dealer in rare books of all kinds, and an author and publisher of some note. But he also was one of those outlandish characters that only Texas among the states seems capable of producing, and when I read a brief wire service account of his death, I immediately asked the Dallas Morning News state editor, Donnis Baggett, if I could go to Bastrop. Almost everything that ever had happened to John Jenkins had been extraordinary. I was sure that his death was extraordinary, too. As of this writing, in October 1992, no arrest has been made in the case.

LAS VEGAS REMEMBERS JOHN HOLMES JENKINS III AS A HIGH-STAKES player, a regular on the poker tournament circuit and a $100,000 winner in the Amarillo Slim tournament just two months ago.

But in Texas, where Mr. Jenkins was famous for his brilliant historical scholarship and passion for rare books, he faced financial ruin, Bastrop County Sheriff Con Keirsey said.

"They were jerking the rug out from under him," Sheriff Keirsey said. "One bank in Austin has a judgment against him for $600,000. His business property is being foreclosed on. The IRS was about to audit him. He owed a Las Vegas casino $20,000. He has other gambling debts. His whole world is crashing."

Mr. Jenkins, 49, also carried between $2 and $4 million in life insurance, the sheriff said. "The family's attorney said the two-year exclusion period on suicide was past. The family said most of the insurance was to satisfy lenders, banks and so forth."

Whether any of this is the reason Mr. Jenkins was found floating in the Colorado River on April 16 with a bullet through his brain remains anybody's guess. Sheriff Keirsey thinks maybe it is. Mr. Jenkins' widow, his teenage son and his colleagues in the rare-book business think it isn't. Bastrop County Justice of the Peace Bill Henderson has issued a ruling supporting the family's opinion.

Based on his analysis of the path of the fatal bullet and the fact that no death weapon or suicide note was found, Judge Henderson ruled the shooting a homicide.

"Given the lack of evidence at the scene that it was a suicide, I had no alternative," he said.

But Sheriff Keirsey calls the ruling "misinformed."

"The angle of the bullet is completely compatible with suicide," he said. "We know the trajectory of the bullet. It's measurable. It's physics. But due to the lack of a weapon, I can't really argue with Judge Henderson. He almost has to call it a homicide."

Johnny Jenkins, as his friends called him, was one of the best-known dealers in rare books and rare historical documents in the United States. He was one of the foremost experts on Texas history — particularly the period of the Revolution and the Republic — and had edited a 10-volume work titled *Papers of the Texas Revolution*. He had written several books, including *Basic Texas Books*, considered an outstanding reference work on Texana, and an autobiographical account titled *Audubon and Other Capers*. His company, the Jenkins

Co., had published more than 300 books, most of them concerning Texas and Southwestern history.

He also was one of those flamboyant, more-vivid-than-life characters that often come to people's minds when they think of the word "Texan." He embellished his 5-foot-6, 160-pound frame with a 10-gallon hat and cowboy boots, smoked big cigars, loved a good story, drank bourbon and played poker. Like "Amarillo Slim" Preston and "Texas Dolly" Brunson, he had been given a nickname in Las Vegas. The players called him "Austin Squatty."

"He was in action all the time," said Jim Albrecht, manager of the card room at Binion's Horseshoe, one of 23 Nevada casinos where Mr. Jenkins held lines of credit.

"He did a lot of wheeling and dealing, and he came out pretty good a lot of times," Mr. Albrecht said. "If he had money problems, he kept it very well concealed."

The Rev. Kenneth Kesselus, the Episcopal priest in Bastrop and the dead man's cousin, agrees that Mr. Jenkins loved the game and was good at it.

"Texas boys have grown up for 150 years playing poker. Poker is one of our sports," Mr. Kesselus said. "And for John, it was a sport. It was an adventure. His whole life was an adventure."

Friends also speak of his "genius," his photographic memory and his lifelong, passionate interest in Texas history. Mr. Kesselus had been collaborating with Mr. Jenkins in the research and writing of a biography of Gen. Edward Burleson, an ancestor of theirs who was one of the commanders of the Texas Army during the Revolution and who later served as vice president of the Texas Republic.

Mr. Jenkins had worked on the project off and on for more than 30 years. "Burleson was John's boyhood hero, rather than Roy Rogers or somebody the rest of us would have had," Mr. Kesselus said.

On that fateful Sunday, Mr. Kesselus said, his cousin set out in search of the abandoned graveyard where James Burleson — the father of the general — was buried. Later that afternoon, the Bastrop County Sheriff's Department received a call from a fisherman about a gold Mercedes-Benz that apparently had been abandoned near a public boat ramp under the bridge that crosses the Colorado River on FM969, about six miles west of Bastrop.

"When the deputy, Jim Burnett, went down there and was looking at it, a couple of guys and a lady were there fishing," Chief Deputy Lee Conner said. "One of the guys cast his line and snagged his hook on the dead man's shirt."

The body was in the river, only about 20 feet from the car. Mr. Jenkins' clothing was entangled with the branches of a broken willow lying in the water, near the bank. A large-caliber bullet had entered his head from behind the right ear and had exited through the left temple, blowing away a portion of the brain and skull.

Sheriff Keirsey insists that he hasn't dismissed the possibility of murder. Thorough searches of the river bottom with a powerful magnet and a metal detector have failed to find the weapon used to kill Mr. Jenkins. But, the sheriff says, the death scene troubles him.

"All our physical facts do not indicate a second party was there," he said. "Jenkins' billfold was found right beside the car. It was void of the driver's license and credit cards and any cash, but the other papers were all still neatly in place. There were no indications of a hasty search-through like the common thieves normally do. Jenkins' gold Rolex watch was missing, but the car wasn't ransacked or rifled through.

"There was no ground disruption, no evidence of struggle, no sign that the body had been dragged to the water."

What bothers the sheriff most is the nature of the shooting itself.

"The Travis County medical examiner says the type of wound and the trajectory of the bullet are compatible with self-infliction," he said. "The gun was firmly pressed to the flesh. . . . If a second party was involved, he probably would have been shot from some distance. The bullet would have followed a different trajectory. There would have been some ground disturbance, some sign of a struggle or a dragging of the body.

"Matter from the head exploding would have been splattered on something," he said. "We didn't find a speck or drop of anything."

Sheriff Keirsey speculates that Mr. Jenkins was standing in the river when the shot was fired. "I think he was three or four feet out into the water, maybe waist-deep," he said. "If somebody else did it, he went into the water with Jenkins and waded back out. But there was no sign of anybody coming out of the water."

The weakness in the suicide scenario is the absence of the death weapon. A sweep of that area of the Colorado River with a powerful magnet soon after the body was found turned up the keys to the Mercedes, but no gun. Last weekend, divers spent six hours combing the river with an underwater metal detector. They turned up a pocket watch, several pieces of Reed and Barton silver flatware, three golf clubs, a plastic bag full of bullets and even a Rolex watch, but no gun. The Rolex didn't belong to Mr. Jenkins.

"There are lots of us in Bastrop County and Austin who would like to know why the sheriff hasn't dismissed suicide as a possible cause of death," Mr. Kesselus said. "He was out there looking for the grave of James Burleson, and somebody killed him."

But Sheriff Keirsey said two acquaintances of Mr. Jenkins' had told officers that Mr. Jenkins occasionally discussed — in a hypothetical way — the possibility of a person committing suicide and making it look like murder. When an article mentioning Mr. Jenkins' suicide comments was published in the *Austin American-Statesman* last week, the sheriff's department received several calls from the public suggesting how such a suicide might be committed.

"The favorite method they've come up with," Deputy Conner said, "is you punch a few holes in a plastic Coke bottle and tie it to the gun. You wade into the river and shoot yourself. The gun drops into the water. The Coke bottle keeps it afloat while it drifts downstream. Then, when the bottle fills with water, the gun drops to the bottom, maybe half a mile from the scene."

Some of Mr. Jenkins' acquaintances dismiss as "absurd" the idea that he would commit suicide as a way out of his financial difficulties.

"I guess that's the only word for it," said Kevin MacDonnell, an Austin rare-book dealer who used to work for Mr. Jenkins. "Such a thing was against John's very nature. The most remarkable characteristic about him was his ability to pull a rabbit out of the hat, to overcome adversity, to find ways around problems."

The public became aware of Mr. Jenkins' intelligence while he was still young. When he was 14, he discovered the memoirs of an ancestor, John Holland Jenkins, who at age 13 had served in the Texas revolutionary army. His reminiscences of early Texas had been published piecemeal in the weekly *Bastrop Advertiser* during the 1880s. The young Jenkins edited them into a continuous narrative, added footnotes and an appendix, and took his manuscript to J. Frank Dobie, the potentate of Texas letters.

Mr. Dobie not only read the book and recommended its publication by the University of Texas Press, but he also provided the foreword, in which he wrote, "Many a Ph.D. thesis shows less scholarship and less intelligence than Johnny's editorial work and is not nearly so interesting."

The young author titled the book *Recollections of Early Texas*, and he received the first published copy on the day he graduated from high school in Beaumont. Later that year, when he entered the University of Texas at Austin, the book was assigned to him in his history class as a collateral text.

Mr. Jenkins always claimed that it was Mr. Dobie — and UT-Austin President Harry Ransom and historian Walter Prescott Webb — who encouraged him to go into the rare-book business.

In 1975, he pushed ahead in that business in a big way — by buying the famous Eberstadt Collection of Western Americana for $2.7 million. At the time, it was the largest single purchase of rare books ever made. Mr. Jenkins sold it, piece by piece, for more than $10 million and established himself as a major player in the rarefied world of rare-book dealing and collecting.

During the 1970s and early '80s, Texas was enjoying an immense economic boom and — largely through Mr. Jenkins' efforts — a growing number of Texas millionaires began investing in rare Texas books and documents, driving their value upward. Mr. Jenkins was acknowledged to be the top expert in the field.

But on Christmas Eve 1985, a fire destroyed an estimated $3 million worth of rare materials — many of them uninsured — in his

Austin warehouse. The cause of the fire was ruled to be faulty electrical wiring. In 1987, after Mr. Jenkins had moved his business to another location, a second fire destroyed an estimated $100,000 worth of his stock. The fire was ruled arson, but no arrests were made.

Meanwhile, W. Thomas Taylor, another Austin rare-book dealer, discovered that forged copies of famous Texas documents — early printed copies of the Texas Declaration of Independence and Col. William B. Travis' famous "Victory or death" letter from the Alamo — had been sold to a number of important institutions and prominent people, including the Dallas Public Library, the museum at the San Jacinto battleground, the Star of Texas Museum at Washington-on-the-Brazos, Gov. Bill Clements and the Barker Texas History Center at UT-Austin.

Mr. Jenkins wasn't the forger, but he had sold a number of the fakes.

"I hadn't yet come to the university when the two fake documents were purchased from John Jenkins," said Dr. Don Carlton, the Barker Center's director. "But if I had been here, I would have bought them, because they were so good. They were excellent pieces, but they were fake. When it was determined that they were fakes, Jenkins immediately reimbursed us."

Whether or not Mr. Jenkins knew the documents were forgeries when he sold them, the discovery blemished his reputation.

And, like nearly every Texas wheeler-dealer, Mr. Jenkins was deeply damaged by the slump in the state's oil economy. He defaulted on a number of loans, including one for $1.3 million — with two partners — for the purchase of an oil rig in West Texas and several loans to renovate the campus of defunct Westminister College near Mexia, Texas, which he bought for $55,000 in 1977.

Nevertheless, Mr. Jenkins' friends don't believe that he would be driven to take his life by such a mundane problem as money.

"Someone saw him alone and decided to rob him," said his cousin, Mr. Kesselus.

"I can't imagine that John ever in his life faced anything that he didn't think he could overcome," said Mr. MacDonnell, the Austin rare-book dealer.

Sheriff Keirsey shrugs.

"Jenkins wasn't the type of person who would commit suicide out of despair. But there's another type that most people don't reckon with. This is the flamboyant-type person with a high intellect."

If Mr. Jenkins' death indeed was a suicide, Sheriff Keirsey believes, he would have wanted to make it look like a murder.

"He was a sixth-generation Texan," the sheriff said. "His family is steeped in history and tradition. That man would not want to stigmatize his name."

April 1989

TRUCKING

When I was researching this story, I drove all over the Dallas-Fort Worth area looking for women driving pickups. I couldn't find any, so I went ahead and wrote the piece without women in it.
It was a big mistake, of course. As soon as it was published, I started getting letters from female pickup fanatics who were offended that they weren't represented.
I'm still sorry.
I apologize again.

"If you've got a good truck with a good engine and a good rear end in it, you can go anywhere, haul anything and pull anything," said Hollis McFail, a cowboy from Bonham, voicing the sentiment of multitudes.

Mr. McFail's own 1983 Ford F350 had pulled the trailer containing his roping horse and saddle to the Mesquite Championship Rodeo. The truck is a "dualie," meaning it has four wheels in the back, like a semi. A "dualie" is a serious truck. "This old truck will take you straight down the road," Mr. McFail said. "This old dun here" — he stroked his horse's withers — "me and him have been down the road a bunch of times in this old truck, and it has never let us down."

Another day, Ocie Allen was standing beside his 1989 GMC 8500 in the parking lot of a North Fort Worth cafe where he had come to get some tamales before he started home. Mr. Allen raises Angus cattle between Denton and Decatur. "A truck is a necessity for me," he said. "Like today I had to come to Fort Worth for some cattle minerals. You can't haul cattle minerals in the trunk of a car."

He has no special feeling for the GMC, he said. It's just a tool, just one of a long line of pickups that have served him over the years, not particularly better or worse than the rest. "But I couldn't run my place without it," he said.

Listening to Mr. McFail and Mr. Allen stirred long memories in my mind, of bouncing along rough ranch roads in a battered old pickup, jumping out to open the gates for the battered old cowboy driving it, hauling horses or hay or blocks of salt, or checking the tanks after a big rain. In my pickup memories, it's always sundown, and the air is redolent with sage in bloom. Sometimes I got to drive and somebody else had to open the gates. That was glory.

Texas was a rural state then. Most of us lived in the country or in the little farm and ranch and oil and sawmill towns. Pickups were for the work of those places, as Mr. McFail and Mr. Allen use theirs now. They rarely were driven for pleasure. "If I was just going for a ride," Mr. McFail said, "I'd rather go in a car."

Now nearly all of us live in cities. We no longer have daily dealings with horses and cattle minerals and hay or anything else that needs hauling or pulling. Yet Impact Resources, a research firm that keeps track of such things, says Dallas-Fort Worth is tied with Sacramento, Calif., for second place in the percentage of residents whose primary car is a pickup. And in first place? San Antonio.

Add in the number of urban Texas families who own a pickup as a second or third or fourth car, and you've got . . . well, you've got a lot of trucks. You see them on every street, in the parking lots of shopping malls and office buildings, even racing the Bentzes and BMWs and Porsches up the Dallas North Tollway.

Why?

Mr. Allen shrugged and kind of smiled. "I don't know," he said. "Maybe everybody wants to be a cowboy. Also, everybody likes to have something to haul things in."

Ray Adler is a business executive, the head of a Dallas public relations firm that he founded. He didn't grow up on a farm or ranch. He has never worked with horses or cattle. He isn't even the son of a truck-owning family. But he had just bought a 1991 extended-cab, four-wheel-drive Chevrolet Silverado 1500. He thinks it's the sixth or seventh truck he has owned.

"I'm not real sure why I have to have a pickup," he said. "I don't haul anything. I do a little hunting and camping, and I sort of tell myself that's what the truck is for. But it isn't really. My wife says it's a throwback to little boys wanting a wagon. She not only won't drive it, she won't ride in it."

Mr. Adler's truck isn't like the pickups I used to know. Those had worn-out seats with busted springs covered with pieces of old quilts or saddle blankets. Their cabs were full of wrenches, hammers, wire-cutters, a rifle or two, boxes of .22 and .30-.30 cartridges, wadded up empty cigarette packs, old feed store receipts and other bits of paper covered with pencil-written numbers, coils of rope, hanks of baling wire, and nuts and bolts that rolled about the floor and banged against the door. Their beds carried pieces of windmills, shovels, crowbars, posthole diggers, little piles of old hay and cottonseed cake, more hanks of baling wire, a couple of empty tow sacks, the excrement of sick calves and sometimes a dog. Their windows were cracked. Their fenders were torn and dented. No one had ever thought of washing, much less of waxing them.

There isn't a speck of dirt on Mr. Adler's brightly polished truck. The seats are of red velour. Red carpet covers the floorboard. It's air-conditioned. It's equipped with power steering, power brakes, a tilt steering wheel, cruise control, a stereo, a telephone, and a ham radio. The bed is protected by a bed liner, which is so clean that surgery could be performed on it.

"You should have seen the one I just got rid of," Mr. Adler said. "It was a four-door crew cab. You could haul six huge oilfield workers in it if you wanted to. It was so long it looked like Moby Dick parked in the driveway. My wife kept saying, 'When are you going to sell that truck?' One day this young man rang my doorbell and said, 'You have a truck in the driveway, and I'd like to buy it.' I said, 'Son, that truck is my pride and joy. Go away and leave me alone.' He came back two or three times. Finally he persuaded me to let him take it away.

"Why I ever got that truck, I don't know," he said. "It seemed like the right thing to do at the time."

He sighed. "The thing about having a pickup," he said, "is that all your friends remember you when they've got something to haul."

Lynn Hearn and his son Kyle saw the raggedy 1951 Chevrolet at a swap meet in February 1988. It belonged to a farmer from near Duncan, Okla. The Hearns bought it for $1,000 and brought it home to Bedford and began to restore it.

Now it's bright blue and shiny enough to make you squint. It has every authentic accessory that the Hearns could find at their swap meets — chrome spotlight, chrome hood guide, chrome bumper guard, deluxe heater, windshield washer, even one of those outside sun visors that sticks out over the windshield like the bill of a cap, and a traffic light finder that helps the driver see out from under that visor. The original 1951 Texas state inspection sticker is still on the windshield. A genuine 1951 Texas license plate is on the front bumper.

The Hearns' pickup is the same vintage as those I used to bounce across the ranches in, but none of them ever was as beautiful as theirs, even when it was new. Whenever Kyle takes it out for a spin other drivers call to him: "Trade you!"

"It's very satisfying to take would-be junk and bring it back to where it's dependable and still usable and people admire it," Lynn Hearn said. "To me that truck is a testimony that at one time the people of the United States built something that was worthwhile, with integrity, that lasted. It didn't just disappear. You could rebuild it. But you can't take a modern car apart and rebuild it even if you want to. This truck is simple. If it quits on you, it can't be anything but the electrical or the gas. If a modern car quits on you, it's the computer or the mass air flow sensor or the crank sensor, and without the right equipment you can't find out what it is."

"It's a neat old truck to drive," Kyle Hearn said.

Unfortunately, a modern city isn't a safe place to drive a masterfully restored antique in which a year of time and labor and thousands of dollars have been invested. "I can't drive it much anymore because people open their car doors and bang them into it," Kyle Hearn said. "I've already got two or three little dings on the fender. So I just drive it to car shows now."

"People just don't respect other people's property and other people's sweat," Lynn Hearn said.

David Owens of Pleasant Grove has to be careful with his truck, too. He can't keep it where he lives because he fears it might be stolen.

It's a 1950 Ford. He paid $750 for it and says he has put $10,000 into it during the 15 years he has owned it. Unlike the Hearns, who restored their truck to what it originally was, only better, Mr. Owens has spent his time and money making his pickup into something new and unique. It has become his life work.

"I've owned many cars," he said, "but I always wanted an old truck. When I started looking, I ran into this old Ford in South Dallas. I didn't even know the guy. I went up to his door and asked him, 'Is that old truck out there for sale?' And he says, 'Yeah, it's for sale.' And I says, 'How much you want for it?' And he says, 'Seven and a half.' And I says, 'You got a title for it? Go get it.' And he says, 'Don't you want to see how it runs?' And I says, 'I don't care how it runs. I'm ready to buy it right now, and I have the money right here in my pocket.'"

He took the grille off and chromed it. He painted it a beautiful red. He put a Mustang engine in it, then changed his mind and put another engine in it, then changed his mind. . . . "I've had this thing in pieces so many times," he said.

He spoke of all the work he has done on it over the years. The memory of every engine, every transmission, every differential, every modification of the chassis is vivid in his mind. "I've never had nothing that draws the attention that this old pickup does," he said. "People keep flagging me down, wanting to stop so they can look at it. The old truck drives, man. It's got power steering, power brakes, tilt wheel, electric seat. It's got everything, boy."

He has vowed never to sell it. "When I die, my brother is going to get it," he said, "and when he dies, my daughter will get it." His daughter is nine now.

"You've got to keep something in life," he said. "I couldn't keep a wife, and I couldn't keep my money, and I couldn't keep a lot of other things. But I'm going to keep my truck."

I asked him if he ever hauls anything in it. He looked at me as if I had shot his dog. "Haul anything!" he said. "Naw!"

Plato wrote that each of us is born with only half a soul. We spend our lives searching for the other half, which is housed in the body of another person. Only when we find our soul mates can we be truly happy.

John Davis found Ernie in 1979 and bought him for $300. Over the years their relationship has become, well, mystical. "One day Ernie wouldn't start," Mr. Davis said. "I couldn't figure out why. Finally, I walked over and looked at the right front tire, something I wouldn't ordinarily do. It was flat. So I put some air in the tire and got back in and cranked it again, and Ernie fired right up. He was trying to tell me something was wrong. He has ways of communicating with me."

Mr. Davis is an Oak Cliff artist who makes designs to be printed on T-shirts. Ernie is a 1960 Ford F100. Ernie Ford. Get it?

"I bought Ernie primarily to haul two broken motorcycles around in," Mr. Davis said, "but I have used him for everything. I used him to haul away an entire fence that went around my granddad's house. Ernie got it all to the dump in one trip. I've used him to pull trees down. I put a Volkswagen in the back of him one time. I guess the biggest task he ever performed was retrieving my wife's big old Oldsmobile from Salado, Texas, a couple of years ago. Ernie's rear end caught fire near Waxahachie. Since then, when I get him up to about 45 miles an hour, his rear end starts going: 'OOOOoooooOOOOOooo, huhuhuhuhuhu HUHU HUHU huhu, ooooooOOOOOooooo.' I've camped out in Ernie. I've lined his bed with plastic and filled it with water for a makeshift hot tub."

Ernie was sitting in Mr. Davis' driveway alongside a 1973 Ford 360 that Mr. Davis also owns. The newer truck had a dead battery, but Mr. Davis didn't care. "That one isn't half the truck Ernie is," he said. "I haven't even bothered to name it. I haven't even figured out what gender it is."

He patted Ernie on the hood. "Doesn't this truck kind of have an aura about him?" he said proudly. "A lady in the fashion business saw Ernie once and said, 'Oh, how darling! It has a patina!'"

"Patina" is a kind word for Ernie's complexion, which is mostly dark green — apparently his original color — with splotches of blue, black and a pinkish tint that may be his undercoat. His windshield and windows are cracked. His junk-filled bed is covered with a topper of a different green, borrowed from Ernie's 1973 companion. A DANGER sign attached to Ernie's grille doesn't seem a joke.

"Ernie offends people," Mr. Davis said. "My dad hates him. The first time he ever saw Ernie, he said, 'Anybody hurt in that wreck?' Ernie and I have been in trouble many times. He's such a bad beast."

Mr. Davis told of an incident in his earlier days when he was dating a girl who lived in Highland Park. He and Ernie were helping her move. "I parked in front of her place and unloaded her stuff," Mr. Davis said. "The neighbors were peeking through their blinds at Ernie. Others came out of their houses on the pretext of checking their mailboxes. I said in a real loud voice, 'Thank you, ma'am. I'll call you tomorrow.' Then I grabbed my girl and gave her a big old kiss, then jumped in Ernie and burned off. The neighbors just stood there with their mail in their hands. My girlfriend never got to know them."

Another time, the Highland Park police stopped Mr. Davis and Ernie just to see what they were up to. In an attempt to make Ernie less conspicuous in the neighborhood, Mr. Davis painted "Izod" on his tailgate. When Izod shirts went out of style in Highland Park, he painted the word over and substituted with "Polo."

"Come on," Mr. Davis said. "Ernie and I will give you a ride."

We crawled in, and Mr. Davis cranked the engine. It made a noise like ball bearings rolling down a stovepipe, then belched to life. "Hurray! Ernie lives!" Mr. Davis cried.

Ernie lurched down the driveway and veered into the street. He coughed, groaned, whined, like an old man awakened from his nap before he's ready.

As he gained speed, the ghostly singing that Mr. Davis had described issued from the differential. "Ernie's not running too good," Mr. Davis said. "His carburetor is screwed up." Ernie smelled like Texas City blowing up. When we returned to his house, Mr. Davis shifted into reverse and drove up the driveway backward. Ernie sounded like an armored personnel carrier revving. When we stopped, smoke was drifting from under his hood.

"Why do you love Ernie so much?" I asked.

"It's something about the amount of work we've accomplished together," Mr. Davis said. "It's like having a pal. When I think of all the man hours of work that Ernie and I have done together, all the things we've hauled and pulled . . . I have a ridiculous attachment to Ernie. I don't really know why. I just do. Every day I've driven Ernie has been an adventure."

I hadn't driven a pickup in many years. I wondered if it would be as much fun on the Dallas North Tollway and the LBJ as on the rough, winding ranch roads of my sundown-and-sage memories. On a scorching summer day I phoned Rent-A-Jalopy and asked the lady what kind of trucks they had for rent.

"They're just plain-Jane trucks," she said.

"Are they air-conditioned?"

"They're just plain-Jane trucks," she said. "No frills."

I arranged to rent one for a week. It set me back $175, but when I went to pick it up, my heart soared with joy.

It was an orange-and-white 1974 Chevy Cheyenne with a GMC grille and a Cadillac hood ornament. A Dallas Cowboys sticker and a KPLX 99.5 sticker adorned the rear bumper. A six-inch crack zagged down the driver's side of the windshield like a lightning bolt, and a big round pockmark, made by a rock or a small-caliber bullet, marked the passenger side. The rear fenders were lacy with rust. An orange traffic cone and a couple of tree branches with dead leaves lay in the bed. The cab smelled of dust. The seat was worn and covered with a plaid cloth, which also was worn.

I knew that truck. It was a descendant of the pickups in my memory. I turned the key. The engine came to life without complaint. I turned on the radio. It was tuned to one of the country stations.

George Strait was singing *Does Fort Worth Ever Cross Your Mind?* Oh my. Perfect.

I drove the LBJ. I drove the Tollway, windows down, hot wind in my face, looking down in disdain from my perch high above the peasants in their BMWs. I suddenly knew why so many city people love pickups: Driving one is like being a horseman among pedestrians, like being a cowboy among sissy dudes.

I drove to Keller's on Northwest Highway and parked under the awning with the other pickups and ordered a cheeseburger and fries and a Bud. I listened to the music of my radio, wishing I had something to haul.

"If this truck were really mine," I thought, "I would name him Darrell, and he would never let me down."

November 1990

FREEDOM FIGHTERS

One day I was driving along U.S. 90 just outside of Brackettville, Texas, and saw a sign: SEMINOLE SCOUT CEMETERY, with an arrow pointing off to the left. On an impulse, I turned and drove the country road out to the graveyard. It was a well-kept little cemetery of the type I want to be buried in someday - just the graves, covered with native grasses, with a fence around them. Many of the tombstones were military, with non-military stones grouped around them in families. Four of the stones belonged to winners of the Medal of Honor, our country's highest military decoration. I decided to find out more about the Seminole Scouts.

There was a big stir in the press back in 1988 when Lee Young Jr., was made a Texas Ranger. He was the first black man ever to pin on a Ranger badge, everybody said, the first black ever to be elevated to that elite and legendary corps.

But one of his friends just laughed. "Hell, you're not the first *black* Ranger," he said. "You're the first *Indian* Ranger."

Sergeant. Young laughs, too, telling the story. "I like that," he says.

Actually, both the friend and the press were correct. Sgt. Young, who serves at the Texas Department of Public Safety station in Garland, is a Black Seminole, a descendant of black people who refused to be slaves and became Indians instead.

"The old folks would tell us stories about them," Sgt. Young says. "About all we had, history-wise, was the stories that had been passed on from generation to generation. Just the old people talking about what they heard from their fathers and grandfathers. They were stories about their lives and the things they endured."

But one day not long ago in a secondhand bookstore, Sgt. Young picked up a volume about Indian scouts who had served with the U.S. Army. He opened it. There was a photograph of his great-grandfather, Benjamin July, standing with several other Black Seminoles, gazing solemnly at the camera.

"I bought the book," Sgt. Young says. "I took it home and showed it to my son. My son took it and showed it to his teacher. And the teacher said, 'We need to get your father over to speak to our class sometime.'"

What the children heard was a story not often told, of a fight for freedom that lasted more than 100 years, of an odyssey comparable to that of the Children of Israel from Egypt, and a proud history in danger of being forgotten, even by the descendants of those who lived it.

The odyssey ended on the West Texas frontier, at the place where the Rio Grande flows out of the Big Bend, meets the Pecos and the Devil's River, and then resumes its journey south toward the Gulf of Mexico, the place where Del Rio and Brackettville now stand. It had begun more than a century earlier in the British colonies of Georgia and the Carolinas.

Early in the 18th century a few slaves were escaping from the cotton plantations in the colonies and making their way into Spanish

Florida, where the dense jungles, high grass, venomous reptiles and clouds of insects gave them refuge. About the same time, remnants of the Creek Nation who were unwilling to accept the white man's way fled to Florida, too.

The Creeks who stayed behind called these malcontents "seminole," which was their word for "runaway" or "rebel." Soon the runaway Creeks were thinking of themselves as a separate tribe. They got along better with their fellow fugitives than with their own kinsmen. They intermarried and formed alliances with the runaway Africans, who also started considering themselves Seminoles.

The slave owners were infuriated that just beyond their borders lived free black people raising their own cattle, riding their own horses, tending their own gardens, carrying guns and traveling long distances whenever they chose. Communities of free blacks so near by, they believed, would inspire other blacks to try to escape. If they were allowed to remain free, the Black Seminoles could become a threat to the whole slave system. But their former owners couldn't invade the Spanish colony to get them back.

In 1821, Spain — which had forbade slavery in its colonies — ceded Florida to the United States. Almost immediately, bands of white Americans and Creeks launched expeditions from Alabama and Georgia to try to capture the escaped slaves and place into bondage the younger generations of Black Seminoles who had been born free. But, with the help of their Indian Seminole friends and their knowledge of the Florida wilderness, the blacks repulsed the invaders.

When Congress declared in 1830 that all Indians were to be removed to a reservation west of the Mississippi, the Creeks and the other "Civilized Tribes" of the Southeast submitted and hit the "Trail of Tears" to Oklahoma. But the Seminoles, knowing their black relatives would go into bondage if they obeyed the law, refused to go. When the Army tried, first through negotiation and then by force, to separate the Indian Seminoles from their black friends and kinsmen, it succeeded only in igniting a bloody war.

After 11 years of unsuccessful fighting, Gen. William J. Worth, the commander at the time (and the man for whom Fort Worth later would be named), concluded that the Army couldn't whip the rebels.

"Ten resolute Negroes, with a knowledge of the country, are sufficient to desolate the frontier . . . " one of his aides warned. So the government told the Seminoles that if they would end their resistance, the blacks could go with them to Oklahoma.

In Oklahoma, the government, whose Indian policy was based on almost total ignorance of Indians, immediately blundered. It decided the Seminoles were merely a branch of the Creek Nation and settled them on the Creek reservation. The Creeks regarded them as subject to Creek government and laws, but the Seminoles considered themselves a separate nation. They refused to submit to Creek authority.

Furthermore, the Creeks owned slaves and regarded the Black Seminoles as slaves. When dealing with whites, the Seminoles sometimes called their black relatives slaves, to keep them safe in a land where any free black could be captured and sold into servitude. But selling a black person was against Seminole law, and the Black Seminoles lived in their own villages and were governed by their own chiefs.

The Creeks tried to force the Seminole Nation to disarm its black people and treat them as slaves, but the Seminoles defied them just as they had defied the federal government. Then some of the Creeks claimed that *they* owned the Black Seminoles, and sold fraudulent titles to slave speculators.

When the Seminoles refused to turn over their black tribesmen to the speculators, Creeks and white slave-catchers raided the black villages, captured some of the people and took them away to the slave markets.

Predictably, the U.S. government backed the slavers. "All the difficulties between individuals of the Creek and Seminole nations have grown out of the condition of these slaves," the Army reported to Washington, "and the Negro chiefs have exercised a controlling influence over the Seminoles, and have induced them to resist the government and the laws of the Creek Nation. . . . All of the intelligent Creeks and licensed traders in the nation agree in the statement that these Negroes exercise a most pernicious influence over the Seminoles."

By the winter of 1849, a Seminole chief named Wild Cat and a Black Seminole chief named John Horse were fed up with the Creeks and the government. Together with about 35 Indians and 30 blacks, they stole away from the reservation and crossed the Red River into Texas. In the spring, they crossed the Rio Grande into Mexico, where there was no slavery, and set up camp just south of the river.

A little later, about 200 more Black Seminoles, led by Jim Bowlegs, described by the Army as "an intelligent Negro," started to join Wild Cat and John Horse in Mexico, but an armed party of Creeks and slavers overtook and attacked them. Several Black Seminoles were killed, and most of the rest were herded back to the reservation. But a few escaped and continued on to Mexico. From time to time others would jump the reservation and join them there.

One who made the trek was a teenager named Sampson July, who would become the grandfather of Miss Charles Wilson. She's a retired schoolteacher who lives in Brackettville. She's 82 now.

"Wild Cat said to the Mexican government, 'You just give us some corn and some guns and let us stay where we are, and we'll get rid of the Apaches and Comanches for you,'" Miss Wilson says. "Of course, he might have been drunk when he said it. He was a drunkard. He had a reputation for that. John Horse did, too. We would sit and listen to the old people talk about them. We just listened, and they talked. But the kids don't listen now. They've thrown the history away."

The Mexican government gave the Seminoles permission to stay. In return, they protected the border from Comanches, Apaches and various mad Texans who kept invading Mexico, hoping to establish an empire there. Wild Cat and John Horse were named colonels in the Mexican Army.

"Years later, they moved on farther south about 100 miles, around Nacimiento and Musquiz," Sgt. Young says. "They moved because they were in close proximity to the border, and slavers would cross the border and pick up anyone they wanted and bring them back and put them in bondage. They said, 'Hey, we're too close to Texas. Let's move south.'"

The Seminoles, who eventually numbered a few hundred, proved to be excellent fighters, and they got along well with the Mexicans. But in 1859, a smallpox epidemic killed more than 50 members of the band, including Wild Cat. The Indian Seminoles quarreled over who should succeed him as their chief, and soon they began to drift back to Oklahoma. By 1861, nearly all the Indian Seminoles had left Mexico. But the Black Seminoles, still in danger of becoming slaves if they crossed the Rio Grande, remained.

When the Civil War ended the threat of slavery, some returned to the reservation in Oklahoma. Others moved closer to the Texas border. In 1870, the Army at Fort Duncan, near Eagle Pass, received a letter from the secretary of war, authorizing "the employment of such a number of Indian-Negroes as may be found useful as scouts, provided no more than 200 are kept in service." A few months later, Maj. Zenas Bliss signed up the first seven members of the unit that would become known as the Seminole-Negro Indian Scouts, which would be headquartered at Fort Clark, near Brackettville.

They were in the Army, but they didn't always look like soldiers. They dressed in a modified Indian style. Some even wore buffalo-horn war bonnets into battle. They could speak both English and Spanish as well as their own language, English mixed with West African dialects, called Gullah. They knew the border country in which they were operating, and understood the ways of their adversaries. They could find and follow trails that were a month old across hundreds of miles of desert and mountains. They could ride for days without water. In his reports, Maj. Bliss praised their dependability and described them as "excellent hunters and trailers, and brave scouts . . . splendid fighters."

According to several military historians, never more than 50 Seminole-Negro Indian Scouts served in the Army at the same time. Only 116 in their entire history. But their impact on the Indian wars was immense. Some military historians credit them, more than any other Army unit, with the conquering of the Southwestern frontier.

Between 1873, when a young white lieutenant named John Bullis — who would become their most famous leader — took command of the scouts, and 1881, when the last Indian battle was fought in Texas, the Black Seminoles participated in 26 expeditions against the Comanches and Apaches, ranging from a few days to several months duration. In battle they often were outnumbered six or eight to one. Yet they never lost a man in battle. Never was one even wounded seriously.

After the battle at Palo Duro Canyon in 1874, which finally destroyed the might of Quanah Parker and his Comanches, one of the scouts, Pvt. Adam Paine, became the first of the group to receive the Medal of Honor, the country's highest military decoration.

Seven months later, on April 25, 1875, Lt. Bullis and three scouts — Sgt. John Ward, Trumpeter Isaac Payne and a 16-year-old private named Pompey Factor — attacked a party of about 30 Comanches who had stolen a herd of cattle and were driving it through the desert. The Comanches were armed with Winchester repeating rifles. Concluding that four men with single-shot carbines were no match for such a force, the scouts mounted their horses and were fleeing when they glanced back and discovered that Lt. Bullis had lost his horse, and the Comanches were riding down upon him.

The three scouts rode back under heavy fire, rescued him and escaped. Sgt. Ward, Trumpeter Payne and Pvt. Factor became the second, third and fourth scouts to be awarded the Medal of Honor.

"Bullis and his scouts were quite close personally," University of Texas scholar Kenneth Wiggins Porter has written. "They were more like a large patriarchal family than an ordinary cavalry troop, and Bullis' relationship to the scouts was more that of a war chief to his braves than the conventional officer-men relationship.... This relationship of mutual affection and confidence was inestimably important to the scouts' effectiveness as a fighting organization."

But they weren't treated so well by other whites.

The Black Seminoles believed the government had promised to give them their own reservation in return for their military service. But there was no written record of such an agreement, and despite the efforts of Lt. Bullis and a few other officers who admired the scouts, it never was honored.

And many white civilians along the border, still smarting from the South's loss of the Civil War, hated the Black Seminoles. Scouts caught alone were beaten by white gangs, and criminals led by the outlaw King Fisher murdered three of them in a two-year period.

In disgust, several of the scouts, including Pompey Factor, returned to Mexico, where they had received better treatment, and continued to fight Indians under Col. Pedro Avincular Valdez.

Lt. Bullis eventually rose to the rank of brigadier general; he died in 1911. Three years after his death, the Army disbanded the Seminole-Negro Indian Scouts and evicted them and their families from the military reservation at Fort Clark.

Miss Charles Wilson, who was five years old at the time, is the only Black Seminole still living who remembers their camp beside Las Moras Creek. "We lived in a house with a thatched roof and a dirt floor, like the Mexicans," she says. "But our living room had a board floor, and that's where we took our company. It was the only house in the camp that had a room with a board floor. We were Mexican and Indian. I remember the *metates* that the women used to grind corn on to make our bread."

The Black Seminoles were never given land of their own. Many of them returned to Mexico, as Pompey Factor had done. Others stayed in Texas and became cowboys. As late as 1939, one of the old scouts, Curley Jefferson, was still writing letters urging the government to grant the Black Seminoles some land or some money. His pleas were denied. The Bureau of Indian Affairs had closed the rolls of the Seminole Nation while the Black Seminoles were still in Mexico, and the blacks weren't included on the official list of the tribe. As Indians, the government said, the Black Seminoles didn't exist.

Mr. Jefferson was the last of the Seminole-Negro Indian Scouts to die, in 1959.

"No matter what color you are, you're part of the culture you're raised in," Lee Young says. "We who were born and raised in that part of the country down there around Brackettville and Del Rio, we aren't completely black, and we aren't completely Indian, either. We're a mixture of black and Indian and Mexican. I was raised up speaking Spanish, eating Mexican food, listening to Mexican music. But predominantly, my culture is Indian. That's the way I was raised and taught to do things."

Sgt. Young has always been proud of that culture, he says. When he was a child, his idols were the Lone Ranger and Tonto. "I identified with Tonto," he says.

But not all Black Seminoles have been so proud of their heritage. "When I was small and they told me I was Seminole Indian, I was really ashamed of it," says Lily Mae Dimery. "'Don't call *me* Indian!' I'd say. 'I'm not no Seminole!' The way they talked, the Gullah language that they used, my dad tried to teach it to me, but I didn't want it. I was ashamed of it. I didn't know what the history was, what we had, what it was all about."

Mrs. Dimery, who is 71, is standing with her husband, Louis, and her in-laws, Art and Carol Dimery, in the Seminole Scout Cemetery a few miles outside Brackettville, near the site of the scouts' old camp.

She's gazing at the tombstone of Carolino Warrior, her grandfather. Nearby stands the tombstone of John Shields, the grandfather of the Dimery brothers.

"But it's a thing to be proud of," Mrs. Dimery says. "I just didn't know that then."

Louis Dimery moved away from Brackettville for 30 years and lost contact with his history, too, until he returned in 1972. "Then Miss Charles and Willie, they started talking to me about it," he says.

"Miss Charles" is Miss Charles Wilson, who taught all the Black Seminole children of the Dimerys' generation in a one-room schoolhouse. "Willie" is William Warrior, Lily Mae Dimery's cousin, who works for a trucking company and serves as a reserve deputy sheriff in Del Rio.

"When I was little, I didn't know nothing about the Seminoles," says Carol Dimery. "But Miss Charles, when we was in school, she would tell us stories about them, and we would say, 'Well, tell us more.' But it just went in one ear and out the next. Now that time is going by, she's telling us more, and we're remembering it this time."

When the Brackettville schools were desegregated in 1960, the Seminole Indian Scout Association — a group that Miss Wilson and Mr. Warrior and the Dimerys helped organize — bought their old school building and grounds. "We wanted to keep it for ourselves, because our parents worked so hard to get it for us," Miss Wilson says. Big photographs of Seminole-Negro Indian Scouts hang on the wall near her old school bell.

Now Black Seminoles return to the school from all over the United States and Mexico twice a year to celebrate their history. "We have a celebration on Juneteenth [June 19]," Miss Wilson says, "but that's to honor those Negroes who were slaves. We were *not* slaves. And since we started our organization and are trying to get our people back, we have what we call 'Seminole Days' the third weekend in September. We dance. We sing the old songs. We wear our long Seminole dresses and our turbans. I tell you, we have a good time. On Sunday, we go to the cemetery and have a service in memory of the scouts."

She sighs. "I think the Seminole culture is dying, though, even in Mexico. There are very few of the original Seminoles left down there, because of intermarrying with the Mexicans. That's why the older ones like me are trying to pass something on to the kids."

But much has been lost, she says, because the Black Seminoles always have been reluctant to talk about their lives and history.

"I didn't hear much about the scouts after we left the camp," she says. "The older people just didn't open up. It was their upbringing, I guess. Maybe it's the Indian in them. But after I retired from teaching, I became interested in our history. I give talks here and there. And Willie's getting to the place where he'll open up."

Willie Warrior is 64 years old. He wears the Western hat and boots befitting a lawman on the Rio Grande. When he was in grade school, Miss Wilson was his teacher, and in 1945 he was one of the first two black students to graduate from the 12th grade in Brackettville.

Mr. Warrior is the grandson of Carolino Warrior and the nephew of Curley Jefferson, the last of the scouts to die, and he's a mine of information. He owns a big briefcase stuffed with photographs and documents, and can spin tales for hours.

One by one, he pulls the pictures and the papers from the case and tells a story about each: "When John Warrior enlisted in the service, he stammered. When they asked him his name, he couldn't get it all out. He said, 'Warr . . . Warr . . . Warr . . .' So they wrote him down as 'Ward.' He's buried next to his father, Tony Warrior.

"Back in Florida, everybody had just one name. Like 'July,'" he says. "But it was in Spanish. It was 'Julio.' And my great-grandfather was 'Guerrero,' which means 'Warrior.' 'Guillermo Guerrero' is my name in Spanish. John Horse's name was 'Juan Caballo.'

"You take a black kid or an Anglo kid and raise him in Mexico, he's going to be a Mexican," he says. "You raise him as an Indian, he's going to be an Indian. It's where you're raised, and who you're raised with. Down here on the border, everything bleeds into one."

He pauses for a drink of whiskey. He says he wishes more people would listen. "We try to teach the young ones," he says, "but they don't want to learn. We try to make them understand, but they don't care.

"There were some Seminoles who were *never* slaves, you know. My father traced back our family history, and he could not find a generation of Warriors who had ever been slaves. . . . "

Willie Warrior opens up, deep into the night, telling the stories.

February 1992

JOHN

One of the few people I envy is John Graves. He has lived two of my best fantasies - taking a long canoe trip on a river alone, and finding a quiet, beautiful place away from everybody and living there. He also wrote Goodbye to a River, which I think is the best Texas book of this century. John hates interviews and hemmed and hawed when I asked him. He lately had turned down quite a few people who wanted to write about him, he said. If he let me, somebody might get mad. Let him think about it and call him back in a few days, he said. When I did, he said, "Come on out. I'll talk to you."

On a fall afternoon 35 years ago, John Graves shoved a canoe containing a shotgun, a couple of fishing rods, some camping gear and a dachshund puppy into the Brazos River, then climbed aboard and began paddling south. The day was raw and windy, one of those gray, cut-to-the-bone spells that North Texas can get in November, not the crisp, golden day that he had hoped for the beginning of his journey.

He planned to float from Possum Kingdom Dam, where he had put in, to a spot near Glen Rose, not far above Lake Whitney. As the crow flies, the distance between the two points is only about 60 miles, but as the river flows, twisting like a snake on a hot rock, it's close to 175.

From childhood John had fished and hunted along the Brazos and listened to the stories of what had happened along its banks in the days when the Comanches, who called themselves "The People," held this part of Texas in terror. This stream, which the Spaniards had named "The Arms of God," had become a part of him.

Although he didn't know it yet, he was about to become a part of the river, too. In years to come, when people would think of the river, they would think of John, and when they would think of John, they would think of the Brazos. For this journey was different from the other times that he had spent on the river.

The government had plans to build five new dams between Possum Kingdom and Whitney, turning the part of the Brazos where John was into a string of lakes. So his journey, he thought, would be his last along this beautiful and familiar stretch before it was drowned in its own waters. It would be a farewell journey. He would see the river one last time and say goodbye to it.

John, who was 37 that year, had been away from the Brazos for a long time, living in foreign places. He only recently had returned to Texas, and was revisiting old haunts, trying to regain the familiarness of the things that had gone into the making of him. That was most of the reason for the journey. He hadn't yet thought that he would write a book.

"I had a little scribble notebook," he says. "I would sit down in the evening and write up the day. I was thinking at the time that it would make a good magazine article, and my agent had gotten a commitment and some money from *Sports Illustrated*."

When the three-week-long journey was finished and the article written, *Sports Illustrated* rejected it. "It wasn't sporty enough for them," John says. *Holiday* magazine published it instead. By the time he had finished writing it, John saw that he had put much more into his notebook than the mere facts of his trip. "I became aware," he says, "that I had the material to make a book."

He wrote it and named it *Goodbye to a River*. "In a way, I was trying to explain Texas to myself by writing it," he says. "I was redefining home things. And I liked it. But my experience at that point was only a failed novel or two. I didn't have any great euphoria about its prospects."

It did better than John expected. The critics received it warmly. It was nominated for the National Book Award. And although it lost to William L. Shirer's *The Rise and Fall of the Third Reich*, one of the most popular nonfiction works of the 1960s, John's publisher, Alfred A. Knopf, has kept its hardcover edition of *Goodbye to a River* in print for 32 years now, and Gulf Publishing's paperback edition remains one of the most popular items on the bookstores' Texana shelves.

For many of its readers, *Goodbye to a River* defines Texas, as writing it redefined John's "home things" for him after his absence. It says more eloquently and truly than any other single piece of writing what Texas was and is and is becoming. It reveals — by describing the bitter toil and the bloody conflict and the unforgiving land in which it was created — the Texan soul, without adornment. There isn't a speck of chauvinistic hokum or romantic baloney in his book.

Neither is it parochial or provincial, for it also is about The World and Nature and Life in the way that great literature everywhere illumines these things — by incarnating them in such small, specific creatures as a man and a dog floating down a river.

The journey wasn't particularly dramatic or exciting. Neither men nor beasts nor the elements ever threatened John's safety. He made and broke camp. He caught fish and shot ducks and squirrels and cooked and ate them. He wrote in his notebook and read the books he had brought with him. He had brief, uneventful encounters with other people, but most of the time he was alone.

"We don't know much about solitude these days, nor do we want to," he would write in his book. "A crowded world thinks that aloneness is always loneliness, and that to seek it is perversion. Maybe so. Man is a colonial creature and owes most of his good fortune to his ability to stand his fellows' feet on his corns and the musk of their armpits in his nostrils. Company comforts him; those around him share his dreams and bear the slings and arrows with him. . . .

"But there have always been some of the others, the willful loners. And out alone for a time yourself, you have some illusion of knowing why they are as they are. You hear the big inhuman pulse they listen for, by themselves, and you know their shy nausea around men and the relief of escape. Or you think you do. . . . "

We all yearn for escape and aloneness sometimes, and floating down a river, living off the land and listening to the water and the birds, seems a beautiful thing to do with solitude. Especially when the river is John Graves' Brazos, which in his book isn't just a string of water, but a history as long as the river itself, full of such stone-hard characters as Charles Goodnight and Oliver Loving, Cynthia Ann and Quanah Parker, Bose Ikard, Martha Sherman, Big Foot Wallace and all the blood-loving Comanches and flinty Anglo-Celts who strove against each other.

It was of these and their world — gone now, but not so long gone — that John was thinking while he paddled. "No end, no end to the stories . . ." he would write. His thoughts were the long and deep thoughts of one who is alone but not lonely. And a reason so many love his book is that we imagine that if we were drifting down the Brazos in a canoe, John's thoughts are the thoughts we would have.

Goodbye to a River often is called a classic. When this is done in John's presence, he smiles, pleased that you think so, then says: "We won't know that for a hundred years."

"In the simpler times I knew when growing up in Fort Worth, even we town youngsters had some almost unpeopled pieces of countryside, in the Trinity West Fork bottomlands and elsewhere, that were ours in exchange for a bit of legwork and a degree of *sang froid* toward the question of trespass," John has written in *Self-Portrait, with Birds*, an autobiographical essay. "Later on there were Depression country jobs in summer for a dollar a day and keep — wheat harvest, fence-building and so on — and I can't remember a time when wild live things weren't a part of consciousness and when knowing something about them didn't matter."

John's father ran a men's clothing store in Fort Worth, but had grown up in Cuero, in South Texas, wonderful quail country. John grew up hunting with his father and his uncles. The Trinity bottom, his urban wilderness, was just across the Rivercrest Golf Course from the Graves home on Fort Worth's west side.

After high school, he went to Houston and got a degree in English from Rice. When he graduated, in 1942, the country was six months into World War II. John joined the Marines, became an officer, and, in 1944, shipped out for the Pacific. "I didn't last very long," he says. "I was just starting to think I was about halfway competent when I got bashed by a hand grenade."

He was discharged with a captaincy and a Purple Heart in 1946, went to Columbia University for a master's degree, and, in 1948, became an English instructor at the University of Texas in Austin. In charge of five freshman sections of 30 students each, most of whom didn't care a flip about the language or its literature, John was disillusioned quickly by the academic life. "The main thing I remember is the ungraded themes," he says, "stuck in coat pockets and piled on my mantelpiece. And every time I would look at them, I would feel guilty."

Tortured also by the failure of a brief marriage, and "a powerful but stalled compulsion to write undying prose, and a yen to shake the dust of old Texas from my shoes and roam the world, . . . I fled for solace when I could to the pleasures of forest and stream," he wrote in *Self-Portrait*. Two years later, he quit his job and embarked on what he calls "an unreasonably protracted, pigheaded, impecunious, lone-wolf writing apprenticeship lasting for several years and conducted, in the main, more or less on the move and far from my native region.

" . . . All I wanted was to shuck off a few old guilts and inadequacies, and to see and learn and live a bit while engaged in the belated effort to make my work come right."

His wanderings took him to New York, New Mexico, Mexico, England and finally Spain, where he settled, more or less, for three years. "When I went to Europe in 1953," he says, "I thought I would spend six months in England and France and Italy, picking up a little language, seeing everything I was supposed to. But, hell, I bogged down in Spain. I really think it was because it's like West Texas. I tend to treasure the kind of people that a hard, dry country produces."

Living was inexpensive in Spain, and John was selling enough of his writing to get by. He even had a little motorcycle, and was making all the bullfights. "I was writing mostly fiction then," he says, "most of it for the 'slick' magazines of the day — women's magazines, that sort of thing. I would write a story for the slicks, and then I would write one for myself — some serious thing that I would mail off to one of the little literary magazines. The first short story I had ever written — back when I was at Columbia — had been published by *The New Yorker*, and I was wasting a lot of time trying to write like I *belonged* in *The New Yorker*, which I didn't. Most of the serious stuff was really bad."

He also was contributing semi-regularly to *Holiday*, a popular magazine devoted mostly to travel and good places to be. And he wrote a novel, which he won't talk about. "There's a manuscript stashed down at the Humanities Research Center in Austin with instructions that it can't be opened until 25 years after I'm dead," he says.

"But mostly, I was just living in congenial places. And it was a good life."

In 1957, after about four years abroad, he returned to Fort Worth to visit his family. "I didn't come home because I wanted to," he says. "I just felt that I *ought* to. I never thought I was going to stay."

Once home, however, his life began to change. His father became ill with cancer. John's brief visit became an indefinite stay. He took a job teaching creative writing at Texas Christian University, which offered him a sunnier experience of academia than he had had at the University of Texas. "If you get to teach what you know and like and want to teach, it's fun," he says. "I had bright kids, and they were all there because they wanted to be, which is a lot different from a freshman class."

He met Jane Cole, a young designer for Neiman Marcus, and fell in love. And, in books and the outdoors, he began rediscovering the Texas wildlife and history that had fascinated him in his youth. Eventually he realized he had returned to stay.

"What it amounted to was a homecoming, a re-exploration in adult years of roots and origins, an arrival at new terms with the part of the earth's surface that was and would remain, regardless of all its flaws, more my own than any other part could ever be," he would write years later in *Self-Portrait, with Birds*. "The wandering years, it seemed, had served their purpose. I could now exist where I belonged, chasing echoes, without wondering if there might be better things to chase elsewhere. There weren't, not for me. I'd gone to a good many elsewheres and was glad I had, but I was back home now.

"And without much dark pondering having occurred, the work that I wanted to do fell into place and began to speak in my own voice, for better or worse, of these matters and others."

That finding of his voice might be dated from one afternoon when he sat down at his typewriter and wrote: "They called him Pajarito. . . ." It was the beginning of a story about an encounter between Tom Bird, an old frontier cattleman, and a band of Comanches led by an old warrior named Starlight, who came to Mr. Bird's ranch and asked him to give them a buffalo from a small herd that he kept.

"The story just sort of wrote itself," John says. "I stayed up all night and finished it. It's so wonderful when that happens, and so seldom."

The Last Running was published by *The Atlantic Monthly*, was reprinted in one of the *Best American Short Stories* collections, and has been issued twice in book form. It's widely acknowledged as a masterpiece, and may be the best short story yet about the end of the frontier and the meaning of its loss. *The Last Running* is as hard and tough as the old rancher and his ancient Comanche adversary, completely dry of sentimentality. But its power and the haunting echo of its last sentence — "We had a world, once." — have made many Texans and at least one Indian cry.

A few years ago, a friend of John's bought a copy as a Christmas gift for a grandson of the great Comanche chief, Quanah Parker. John inscribed it to the man, "whose valiant people made my people know they had been in a hell of a fight."

"The old man cried," John says. "You make a Comanche cry, you've done something."

The Comanches were much in John's thoughts during his Brazos journey, for it was along the Brazos that some of the bloodiest collisions between the merciless "lords of the South Plains" and the equally pitiless Anglo-Celtic invaders had taken place.

The Comanches, John would write in *Goodbye to a River*, "ate up the seed corn and the brood stock that were furnished them, converted their tools to arrowheads and battle axes, and on horseback drifted in and out of their reservation pretty much at will. The great Comanche Trail, ancestral route of thievery and rapine, lay near.... Buffalo ... still teemed on the plains to the west. Two centuries of sweet wild tradition urged the Comanche to follow them, to ride and hunt and fight. Hand mirrors and hoes and occasional begged whiskey and strings of colored beads and the stink of a mule's behind were not a fair trade for that."

Their white enemies, on the other hand, "were the cutting edge of a people whetted sharp to go places, to wear things out and move on, to take over and to use and to discard. It is doubtful that any of the people in history whetted in that way . . . have wanted to dwell much in their minds on the humanity of the people in their path, on abstract justice. If they had, they wouldn't have been able to go where they went."

By the time he finished writing his book, John had found not only his voice but the themes that would occupy him for the rest of his career. They would be the land itself, and "the kind of people that a hard, dry country produces."

When he was home about a year, John married Jane, and they lived on a rented country place outside Fort Worth. But John was struck by what he describes as "the incipient disease of the land," the desire to own his own piece of ground. "I had never managed to purge myself of the simple yeoman notion," he would write, "that grass and crops and trees and livestock and wild things and water mattered somehow supremely, that you were not whole unless you had a stake in them, a daily knowledge of them."

A particular spot down in Somervell County had stuck in his thoughts. "A friend of mine started building up a ranch in pieces down here in 1947," he says. "I'd come down with him, camping, and sometimes I'd come down by myself and wander around. In some of that wandering around, I happened onto this place. It was just old, beat-up, used-up land. But it was remote and private, and that was the main thing."

He bought one overgrazed homestead and later added another, giving him almost 400 acres of eroded, cedar-infested limestone hills

— some of the land that the Anglo-Celts had conquered and quickly worn out — with a beautiful creek, close enough to Glen Rose to be convenient, but far enough from the town and the highways. He began building a small stone house on a limestone ledge beside some live oak trees.

"I just intended it as sort of a hunting and weekend cabin," he says. "Jane wasn't interested in the place. She seemed rather indifferent. But about the time I got the cabin built and some of the land cleared of cedar, she decided she wanted to move down here."

As he became more involved in the labor of the land, John found that the focus of his own purpose was changing. The learning of what he calls "yeoman skills" — the clearing of cedar, the building of fences, plowing, the tending of cattle, the enlargement of his house, the construction of outbuildings — began to fascinate him and give him more pleasure than he had imagined possible.

When he and Jane became parents — two daughters, Helen and Sally, were born within the first four years of their marriage — Jane had quit her job at Neiman Marcus. And John's class at TCU met only once a week. So "Hard Scrabble," as he called the place, became the center of their lives, and John evolved into what he jokingly calls a "squireen," a small-time country gentleman.

He quit teaching in 1965. He worked for a while as a writer-consultant with the U.S. Department of the Interior, but for more than 25 years now he has made his living as a free-lance writer and farmer. He has raised some crops and some cattle, but the most valuable harvest that Hard Scrabble has yielded is the writing John has done about the place and his life on it.

In 1974 — 14 years after *Goodbye to a River* — he published his second book, which he named after his farm. *Hard Scrabble*, he wrote, "is not the account of a triumphant return to the land, a rustic success story, but mainly a rumination over what a certain restricted and unmagnificent patch of the earth's surface has meant to me, and occasionally over what it may mean in wider terms."

There surely is no other piece of land in Texas that has been described in such detail as John's place. He describes its terrain, in the middle of what he calls the "Tonkawa Nation," the dinosaurs who left their tracks along the Paluxy River not far beyond his fences, the prehistoric peoples and their Indian descendants who ate mussels from White Bluff Creek, the cattlemen and farmers whose wrongheaded practices stripped the soil of its power and tore the soil itself from its limestone bedrock, the cedar choppers who made their living from cutting the pestiferous trees and selling them for fence posts, the natural plant and animal life of the place, the local hunters of foxes and coons, the poachers of deer and wild turkeys and, of course, the pleasures and frustrations of his own efforts to restore the land and make it productive again.

As in *Goodbye to a River*, his ruminations, as he calls them, move beyond his immediate surroundings to Man everywhere and in every time and his relationship to land and the rest of the natural world.

In 1977, John began writing a series of wise, often humorous essays for *Texas Monthly* about such rustic matters as illegal Mexican laborers, goats, bees, dogs, chickens, weather and the users of chewing tobacco and snuff. In 1980, John collected them into a book called *From a Limestone Ledge*.

In it John acknowledges that his toil on Hard Scrabble hasn't yielded all that he once hoped it would, and that advancing age makes it unlikely all his dreams will be realized. But he faces the truth serenely: "Let there now be contemplation, you tell yourself, contemplation and some placid enjoyment, even if the damned place is still not in shape."

And in *Self-Portrait, with Birds*, he realizes that the most significant accomplishment of his labor has been not on the land, but in his own attunement with nature. ". . . I am relieved and grateful in this later time," he wrote, "to find that the best thing I've acquired in these battered, cedar-clad limestone hills has been not the mastery of yeoman skills, . . . but simple awareness of natural rhythms and ways while living on the land through the seasons' cycle, year by year."

John has published many magazine articles and essays over the years, and a few highly regarded short stories, but it's for this "Brazos Trilogy" — *Goodbye to a River*, *Hard Scrabble*, and *From a Limestone Ledge* — that his name will endure.

Sometimes, he says, three books seem a too-small work for 30 years, but his regret doesn't last long. "I don't think I'd do anything differently," he says. "I keep telling myself that if the place hadn't occupied so much of my time, I would have been more productive, worked more on my writing, but I doubt it. The place became a passion. I didn't think of it as hard work. I loved it all. Except maybe digging the postholes."

The girls are grown and gone. Helen lives in New York now, Sally in Utah. Jane, who went back to work at Neiman Marcus after her daughters left home, has retired. John, approaching his 72nd birthday, has ended his 25 years of labor on the land. He hasn't worked a field in five years. The cedar is taking over again.

"The main thing this place has given me," he says, "is a sense of how everything works together. From the microbes in the soil, to the plants that grow in the soil, to the animals that eat the plants, to the animals that eat the animals, to us. Without really having to depend on it myself, I've learned what dependence on the land means. And I think of that as reality. I'm unable to think of our present civilization as real. The reality to me is what has always been. What works. And the reality is disappearing fast."

The nuclear power plant that has been built just across Glen Rose from Hard Scrabble has changed the economy of once-poor Somervell County. They're building a golf course not far from John's place. Much of the land is owned now by newcomers. But with them, some of the wild animals are beginning to prosper again. "People born in the city, they tend to be a little bit gentler in their attitude toward wildlife," John says. "The original bunch around here, they were hard up, and anything you could eat, they were going to eat it."

He quietly applauds efforts to save endangered species and wilderness and the environment, but he doesn't use his writing to grind those axes. "I grow a little weary of polemics," he says. "It's kind of like sentimentality. It has always tainted my work when I've tried to get involved. And it has a built-in impermanence to it. You've got a cause, and you're fighting for it, and you're putting your writing into its service, and if you win, the writing is obsolete, and if you lose, it's obsolete.

"I decided a long time ago that to be an activist you've got to be optimistic, because you've got to believe something can be done. And there seldom has been anything done."

With Jane and Hodge, their 10-year-old English sheepdog, and a half-dozen steers grazing in the yard, John quietly is living the squireen's life at last, walking his ground, tinkering with his boat, tying flies and indulging his passion for fishing — in his creek, in lakes, in stock tanks, on frequent trips to Florida and the sea off Key West — sometimes with friends, sometimes alone. He corresponds with a few writers and attends an occasional literary gathering. Rarely, he agrees to a lecture or a reading. He scoffs at the reverence in which he's held by other writers and readers. "If you live long enough," he says, "you become an institution."

He has some essays and articles in the works, and lately has been thinking of returning to the form he practiced more than 30 years ago, before *Goodbye to a River* reshaped his future.

"I'd like to write a short novel built around salt-water fishing," he says, "but I haven't figured out exactly how. The trouble with fishing — or any uneconomic passion — is that you get to thinking it matters for its own sake, and it doesn't. If you can't make it matter in human terms, you haven't done anything.

"And I don't have the urgency about writing that I once had, where it was just *digging* at me, you know, and I would start feeling bad if I hadn't written in a while."

As for the river, John's goodbye wasn't final after all. Only one of the five dams that were to be constructed along the Brazos ever got built. During the Carter years, the federal government cut back considerably its funding for such projects. Furthermore, the Brazos water was found to be too salty for use as a municipal or industrial supply.

"I never took the whole trip again," John says. "But for about 20 years after I wrote the book, I would go out on the river. I still go, just for day trips, during the sand bass run in late winter. I'm getting a little stiff for a canoe. After an hour or two, I get kind of cramped up."

And though the river isn't gone, it's no longer the wild place that John and his puppy saw 35 years ago. "There are vacation homes all along the banks now," he says, "and people everywhere. I've had people come up to me and say, 'You ruined the Brazos. You brought all those damn people down here.' Well, they're there. I don't think I did it, though."

"What is, is," he wrote in his book. "What was, was. If you're lucky, what was may also be a part of what is. Not that they often let it be so, now."

June 1992

THE $65,000 FISH STORY

I've always been a lousy fisherman. I try it from time to time, but I've never been able to set my mind to really learn the wily ways of the creatures of the deep and how to catch them. Still, there's an element of luck in the catching of fish, and when one of them has a $65,000 prize tag attached to it... why not give it a shot? Somebody hits the multimillion-dollar jackpot on the Las Vegas slot machine. Somebody wins the Publishers Clearing House Sweepstakes. Somebody who doesn't know what he's doing could get lucky in the Lake Texoma Crappiethon.

HE HAD A DREAM, RAY ZIPPER SAID. "USE A JIG AND PUT A MINNOW on it," the dream told him, "and the fish will come."

"A lot of times I go to sleep with a problem on my mind, and I'll wake up with the answer," Ray said. "I didn't know I had fish on my mind that night, but I guess I did."

He wasn't the only one. All along the shore, from Marietta to Denison, from Tishomingo to Pottsboro, fish were on many minds, for the two-month-long 1990 Lake Texoma Crappiethon was under way. Lurking under the surface of the water, prowling beneath the docks and boathouses, gliding among the branches of drowned trees, resting in the lee of rocky bluffs were 2,196 crappie wearing numbered tags, waiting to bring fortune, fame and happiness to whoever caught them.

Out there somewhere was "Big Bad Buck." He was worth $1,000 to the fisherman who nabbed him, and worth $6,000 if he should be caught with a Buck's Rod from B 'n' M Pole Co. "Bait-A-Hole Betsy" was out there, too. Her prize value would jump from $500 to $1,500 if the angler was using Bait-A-Hole bait from Triangle Products, Inc., at the time of the catch. And "Fintastic Voyager," whose value would jump from $1,000 to $6,000 if his catcher's boat happened to be equipped with a Delco Voyager battery.

There was "Candy Man," worth $25,000 if caught with Crappie Candy bait. And "Crab Claw Clem," worth $40,000 if his captor had a Crab Claw anchor in his boat. And "Kmart Kid," whose captor would be rewarded with $5,000 worth of Kmart merchandise. And "Mighty Minn Kota," worth $40,000 if the angler was using a Minn Kota trolling motor. And 45 other big-money fish. And 2,143 small-fry fish worth $25 each.

And there was "Tangle-Free Tom," the uppermost fish on many minds, the crappie most worthy of a fisherman's dream. His captor would win $5,000, no matter what kind of tackle he used. His value would rise to a dizzying $65,000 should he be caught on a Johnson Country Mile Spin open-faced reel, made by Johnson Fishing, Inc., the Crappiethon's main sponsor.

He was out there somewhere.

But Ray's dream wasn't of any particular fish. After he awoke, he couldn't remember whether the fish in his dream was even wearing a tag.

Ray had paid his $6 entry fee and got his official Crappiethon badge, but the tournament didn't occupy his thoughts much. He lives within a rock-throw of the lake and goes fishing almost every good-weather day, whether there's a tournament or not. But if a fish that he caught should happen to have a tag on it ... well, it would be fine.

The morning that Ray awoke from his dream didn't promise to be a good one for fishing. "The lake was so foggy I couldn't see the water," he said. But he took his boat out and, sitting there in the fog, decided to put his dream to the test. "It seemed like it made sense," he said. "Putting a live minnow on it should make the jig more lively. So I figured I would give it a whirl."

Before long, he had caught four fish. Then he made the strike of his life.

He caught "Kmart Kid." Suddenly he was entitled to $5,000 worth of Kmart stuff.

When I was about six years old, my grandmother took me fishing on a creek near our house. I caught a perch, and my grandmother cooked it for my supper. But we moved to arid West Texas not long after that, and I didn't get much more fishing experience growing up. Just a few catfish caught on trotlines and juglines in the Rio Grande.

I've gone bay fishing on party boats at Port Aransas and South Padre Island, but never caught anything but croakers and stingrays. And when my sons were small, we used to go down to Lake Whitney and throw a few lines off Soldier's Bluff and then fly a kite or throw a Frisbee. Sometimes we would catch a fish or two, but it was always an embarrassment to me that I didn't possess any decent fishing lore to pass on to my boys. I suspected this was a major flaw in a father.

So when Ray invited me to go crappie fishing with him, I had a decision to make: Did I want to display my ignorance in front of a guy who had just caught a $5,000 fish in the fog?

I told Ray I would just watch.

Ray and his wife, Bea, live in a cabin on Preston Peninsula, a few miles north of Pottsboro. He's an X-ray technician and she's an emergency-room nurse. They both work weekends and are off the rest of the week, so they get to fish while Texoma is empty of boaters and water-skiers.

As I drove up the peninsula, I started thinking: What if I were in the boat with Ray and he had an extra rod and I decided that just for the hell of it I would put a line in the water? And what if I caught Tangle-Free Tom and didn't have a Crappiethon badge?

It had happened to a couple of guys already. One fellow caught "Humm Dinger," a $1,000 fish, but hadn't bought a badge and missed out on the prize. Another caught "Fintastic Voyager," then hid him while he hustled off to buy a badge. Half an hour later, he turned in the fish to claim his $1,000 prize. Crappiethon officials, suspicious of such extraordinary luck, demanded that he take a lie detector test, as they had a right to do under the rules of the tournament. He flunked.

I stopped at a tackle shop and bought a badge.

"Need anything else?" asked the man behind the counter.

"Uh, no," I said.

The day was cold and cloudy. It wasn't raining, but it had rained for several days previously. The ground was saturated. The lake was high and muddy. Ray had a new trolling motor on his boat, and a new fish finder with a television screen that showed not only where the fish were, but also the depth and temperature of the water, the speed the boat was moving and the distance Ray had traveled since he left his boathouse. Compliments of Kmart. Including gifts to his wife, his children and his grandchildren, he guessed he had spent half of his $5,000 prize so far.

"I've got no plans for the rest of it yet," he said. "It doesn't seem important. It's all just gravy."

Ray trolled around some submerged brush piles and boathouses. His TV showed fish, but nothing was biting. "A crappie stays close to trees and rocks and structures, and he's pretty passive," he said. "It's known as an old person's fish. It takes a lot of patience to catch a crappie. Sometimes it'll be 30 minutes between bites."

His jig got tangled in a thorn bush near the shore. "That's called a brush bass," he said. "You can catch all of them you want. There's no limit. You want to fish? I've got an extra rod."

I was about to reach for the rod when Ray mumbled, casually, "You've got a fishing license, I guess."

I didn't. "Uh, thanks," I said. "But I'll just watch today."

Ray's rod bent.

"You've got a bite!" I said.

He reeled it in. It was long, skinny and dark. "Rope bass," he said.

Crappie fishing looked easy. The next time I came to Lake Texoma, I promised myself, I would have a license. I would be ready.

"There are 19 million crappie fishermen in America," Ken Clary said. "And we're putting on 42 Crappiethons in 22 states this year. Seven of them are in Texas. We started in Florida in January, and go all the way up north. The last ones are in Minnesota and New York state in June."

Mr. Clary is president of America Outdoors, Inc., of Decatur, Ala. Crappiethon U.S.A., a subsidiary of his company, sponsors the crappie tournaments and publishes *Crappie World*, the crappie fisherman's Bible.

"Forty thousand fishermen in Texas fished Crappiethon last year," Mr. Clary said. "About 300,000 fishermen will enter Crappiethons this year nationwide. There are 20 national sponsors of the tagged fish, plus a lot of local sponsors. Crappiethon U.S.A. gets $4.75 of each $6 entry badge, and the local sponsor who sells it keeps $1.25. The 300,000 fishermen probably will catch about 15 percent of the tagged fish.

"But the 60-day tagged fish tournament is only one part of a Crappiethon. In the middle of it we have a one-day buddy tournament. Two-person teams pay $50 and fish for one day and turn in their top 20 crappie by weight."

Top 20? Was it possible to catch 20 fish in one day? *More* than 20?

"The first prize is $2,000," Mr. Clary said. "But the best part is this: The fishermen in the top three boats get to fish in the Crappiethon Classic in June. This year it's on Smithland Pool, near Paducah, Ky. Our company pays everything except travel expenses. Once the fishermen are there, everything — room and food and drink — is taken care of. It's a one-day tournament and a four-day party. First prize is $40,000.

"Across the country in these one-day tournaments, we'll probably have 9,000 teams, which is 18,000 fishermen. And of those 18,000 fishermen, there's probably 500 or 600 of them who fish in several tournaments, trying to get qualified for that classic."

"What makes a good crappie fisherman?" I asked him.

"Patience," he said. "Patience. And luck."

I remembered clicking through the cable TV channels at odd weekend hours and zipping past guys standing up in boats, not wearing life jackets, holding rods, casting and talking. They caught something almost every time they cast. Bass. It was bass they always talked about. Maybe my neighborhood video store had something that could help me with crappie.

Bass. Almost a whole shelf of bass videos. Half a shelf about trout. Fly casting. Fly tying. Not so much as a snapshot about crappie. Same at the bookstore. Bass. Trout. Flies. Plus philosophical musings by guys wearing rubber pants and standing in crotch-high cold water. Not even a pamphlet about *Pomoxix annularis* and *Pomoxis nigromaculatus*, the two crappie members of the sunfish family, and how to catch them. Maybe patience and luck really were all there was to it.

That night I rummaged in the garage and found my old Zebco Centennial rod and my tackle box. The box contained a knife, my long-ago-expired fishing license, a jar of stink bait, three sinkers and two fishhooks, but with the lid shut it looked as official as anybody else's.

And the hooks were Eagle Claw brand. If I caught "Eagle Ernie" on one of them, I would win $2,000. However, neither hook was an Eagle Claw Automatic rotating hook, which would have paid me an extra grand.

At the first bait store I came to, I bought a new fishing license, then drove on down to Little Mineral Marina & Resort on Preston Peninsula, where I had reserved a cabin. I was signing the register when the guy behind the desk delivered the bad news: "Well, they caught 'Tangle-Free Tom.'"

"No! When? Where?"

"About two hours ago." He pointed out the window. "Right down there at our boathouses, just fishing off the dock."

"Was the guy using a Johnson Country Mile Spin open-faced reel? Did he win the $65,000?"

The man laughed. "Naw, but he said he had one of those in his pickup. He still gets $5,000. I wouldn't cry about that."

Mentally, I kicked myself. If I had arrived 2½ hours earlier, and if I had decided the Little Mineral boathouses were the place to fish, that $5,000 could have been mine. But now that the only two $5,000 fish in the tournament — "Tangle-Free Tom" and Ray Zipper's "Kmart Kid" — had been caught, I stood little chance of coming away from the Crappiethon with more than $1,000.

There was a wall full of fishing lures for sale near the registration desk. I sauntered over to see if any of them resembled the lures I had seen Ray Zipper use. "I need some, uh, jigs?" I said.

The man came over to help me. "A lot of people are using these yellow ones," he said. "Some people like these pink ones, too, but I haven't had any luck with them."

I bought two of each, and a couple of white ones. If nothing else, they would add color to my tackle box.

That night I went to the seminar for one-day tournament contestants at the Pottsboro School cafeteria. Tournament director Jim Climer read the rules to the standing-room-only crowd and announced more bad news. "The lake is six feet above normal," he said. "Texoma is murkier than I've ever seen it. It doesn't even look like Texoma."

Also, he said, eight of the big-money fish had been caught. He introduced Larry Arrington, the Dallas polygrapher who would administer lie-detector tests to the winners, then gave away several thousand dollars' worth of Crappiethon sponsors' products as door prizes.

After the meeting, I introduced myself to Cliff Hayes, the fellow who had yanked "Tangle-Free Tom" from under my nose. I asked him how he did it.

"Well, I got up this morning and went to my spot that I had in mind," he said. "The fish weren't biting real good, but I caught four. The second fish I caught was tagged. Number 2201. I went ahead and caught a couple more, and then I decided to go check that one out. The lady looked in the book for the number, and it wasn't in the book. She called the Crappiethon headquarters in Alabama, and the lady there started asking me all these questions after she checked the number out. Then she said, 'Well, I've got good news and bad news. The good news is, you caught "Tangle-Free Tom." The bad news is, you weren't using the right equipment, so you don't get the bonus.' But I'll take what I got, for sure."

I was sort of hoping he would ask me to be his partner in the one-day competition, but he said he was taking his 15-year-old son, Cliff Jr. So I asked him where they were going to fish.

Cliff Sr. and Jr. exchanged a meaningful glance. "We don't know yet," Cliff Sr. said. "We haven't decided exactly what we're going to do."

"Well, will you tell me what kind of bait you caught 'Tangle-Free Tom' on?" I asked.

"It was a chartreuse jig," he said.

Chartreuse was the only color I didn't buy.

I didn't shell out the 50 bucks to enter the one-day tournament. I didn't have the required partner, for one thing. Ray Zipper, averting his eyes, had told me his wife, Bea, was partnering with him. Anyway, I still doubted it was really possible for anyone — even two people — to catch 20 fish between 6:30 a.m. and 3 p.m., the hours of the tournament. But I was still determined to go fishing. I talked Ray's father, Pat Zipper, into hauling me about the lake in his boat.

I met Pat at 6 a.m. at his boathouse, next to Ray's. Pat and I followed Ray and Bea around the peninsula to a breakwater. Ray anchored, so we did, too. Pat's fish alarm was beeping like crazy.

"Hey! All right!" I exclaimed.

"It's nothing," Pat said. "Just shad."

I assembled my Zebco Centennial and baited my line with one of my new pink jigs. I would have added a minnow to the jig, as Ray was doing, but I had forgotten to get my minnow bucket out of the garage. That meant I couldn't use my Eagle Claw hooks, either.

"I sure hope they don't start biting that," Ray said. "I don't have a thing that's pink."

I tried to cast, but my reel didn't work. I opened it up. The workings had paralyzed during their years of non-use. I had no oil to free them. Pat probably did, but I didn't care for him to know the condition of my equipment. I surreptitiously unwound several yards of line by hand and dropped the jig over the side.

By 7:30 neither Ray, Bea, Pat nor I had so much as a nibble, so we moved on to the Little Mineral boathouses, where Cliff Hayes had caught my $5,000 fish. Nothing happened there, either, so Pat and I decided to split from Ray and try our luck elsewhere. At 10:30 we encountered William Bruno from Wichita, Kan., and his son Paul, from Durant, Okla. They had caught one fish so far.

"Was it worth the drive?" I asked.

"Oh, yeah," William Bruno said. "I just came down to have fun."

Sure. As if there's no water in Kansas.

At 10:55 we ran into Buford Greenwood from Denison and Dennis Reynolds from Sherman. For a while, they pretended we weren't there, so I hollered at them. "Having any luck?"

"Four, so far," Dennis said. "Buford caught a two-pounder."

I threw my jig over the side. Dennie and Buford hauled up their anchor and left, apparently with the only four fish in that part of Texoma.

"Patience and luck, patience and luck," I kept repeating to myself.

By 12:30 I had had all the fun I could stand, so Pat headed his boat back toward his boathouse on the other side of Preston Peninsula. As we were speeding along, a familiar figure hailed us. It was Ray. His boat was broken down, dead in the water. We pulled alongside him.

"A boat is a hole in the water that you pour money into," Ray said. He had caught only one crappie and was going to do the rest of his fishing at his own boathouse. He and Pat lashed their boats together, and we continued our journey.

"Fishing makes for a great marriage," Bea said. "It gets you away from the kids, away from the phone, away from the TV. Sometimes Ray and I sit in the boat and discuss the weirdest subjects for hours."

At 3 o'clock I motored over to the Preston Fishing Camp, where Jim Climer already was weighing in the returning contestants.

Buford Greenwood and Dennis Reynolds were disappointed. Their two-pound crappie weighed in at only a pound and a half. "We just put the big eye on him," Buford said.

"But he looks two, don't he?" Dennis said.

Cliff Hayes Sr. and Jr. had just weighed in. Their best 20 crappie weighed 11.07 pounds.

"How many did you catch in all?" I asked.

"Forty-four," Cliff Sr. said.

"Forty-four!" I shouted. "Where in the world were you fishing?"

"At Little Mineral," Cliff Sr. said. "Where I caught 'Tangle-Free Tom' yesterday."

"But *I* was fishing there!" I said. "I didn't get a bite!"

Cliff Sr. and Jr. exchanged one of those glances.

Louis Kubica of Duncanville and Murray Hatfield of Pottsboro won the $2,000 first prize with 15.40 pounds of crappie. Louis also won the $181.50 second prize in the big-fish pot with a 1.83-pounder. I asked him what makes a good crappie fisherman.

"Patience," he said.

Barney Ross of Oklahoma City and Joe Jesmer of Kingston, Okla., won the $800 second prize with 14.79 pounds. "Patience," Joe said.

"Yeah," Barney said. "Patience."

Peewee Chandler of Gordonville and Bill Smith of Denison won the $500 third prize with 14.45 pounds. Bill also won the $423.50 first prize in the big-fish pot with a 1.93-pounder. This was the second year in a row they've qualified for the Crappiethon Classic.

"What makes a good crappie fisherman?" I asked.

"Well, concentrating," Peewee said. "And using every little trick you know. You've got to concentrate and be dedicated."

"And patience," Bill said. "And a lot of luck."

May 1990

TOWER AMONG FRIENDS

I disagreed with John Tower on almost every political question, but I always liked him as a man. He never beat around the bush with a reporter. He either answered the questions forthrightly, sometimes bluntly, or he refused to answer at all. Although I wasn't eager to see him become secretary of defense in the Bush administration, I thought his confirmation hearings before the Senate Armed Services Committee were mean, treacherous, hypocritical, and a dishonor to the country. In 1991 Tower and his daughter, Marian, were killed in a plane crash.

It could be a high school homecoming. Gray-haired men and women who haven't seen each other in a long time squeal with pleasure, hug one another, shake hands, slap backs and reminisce about the days not so long ago when the Republican Party of Texas could have been convened in a closet with room to spare. They marvel at how time has changed things. More than 200 people — some of them once-powerful pooh-bahs in the Democratic Party who sniffed the political winds and switched allegiance — have paid $50 apiece to gather in an Austin hotel banquet room on a sunny July noon to feel their Republican oats.

With hard work and a little luck and lots of money, they're saying, they can capture the Texas House of Representatives in next year's election. If they do that, they'll be in charge when it's time to redraw the boundaries of the state's congressional districts after the 1990 census. And that would mean more Texas Republicans probably would be elected to Congress.

"It looks like we're going to have a fine slate of candidates next year," says George Williford, who was chairman of the party when the outlook wasn't so rosy. "It's different than it used to be, when we had to dragoon people and hold a gun on them to make them run."

The guest of honor is one of the dragooned, one of the rare ones who got elected. When John Tower entered the U.S. Senate in 1961, he was the first Republican statewide office holder in Texas since Reconstruction, and the first Republican senator popularly elected from a state of the old Confederacy. If the Texas Republican Party has a father, he's it.

After lunch, he rises to speak. "I can remember a time when this many people wouldn't dare to be seen at a Republican function in Austin, Texas," he begins. "It wasn't safe. And it certainly wasn't politically rewarding. . . . "

It's a short, off-the-cuff speech, remembering the old days, urging the party to recruit good people and put up a fight next year. "You can't win a race simply with money alone if your candidate is a turkey," he says. He offers to help. "You can count on me," he says, his voice suddenly rolling like prairie thunder, "because that old political carcass that was hung by a lynch mob from an oak tree in Washington last March has now been cut down and is still alive."

The Republicans stand up and cheer.

Later, several women ask to be photographed with him. "Your reputation may be hereby sullied," he tells them as they pose. "You may wind up in *National Enquirer*."

At midafternoon he boards a private plane and flies on to Tyler for another fund-raiser, this one a $50-a-head reception in the garden of a stately mansion. He spent six years in Tyler during his itinerate boyhood as a Methodist preacher's son, and about 200 of the party faithful have gathered among the begonias and caladiums to greet him. While the katydids scream in the towering oaks, his friends recall old times.

"I've known John since he was just a kid running for the Senate," says Ginny Pearson. "The party was small then, and we did a lot of things, and most of the things we did were wrong."

Mr. Tower and Wilton Fair were Boy Scouts together. "I was a senior patrol leader, and he was a tenderfoot," Mr. Fair says.

Mr. Tower has known some of them almost all his life, but he hasn't been with them in a long time. "Before the end of the evening, I want the old Hogg Junior High bunch to get together and sing our school song," he says.

In the foyer, on an Oriental rug, surrounded by antique Chinese porcelain and women looking worried, a TV crew has set up lights and cameras. The reporter asks Mr. Tower if he's bitter about what happened to him in Washington.

He sighs a small sigh. He has answered the question many times, before many cameras. He's tired of it. "My clergyman father taught me that bitterness and rancor are more destructive to the person feeling them than to the person they're directed against," he says. "So I try to avoid that. Life must go on."

On the plane back to Dallas, Norman Newton, executive director of the Associated Republicans of Texas and ramrod of the fund-raisers, is ecstatic. "What a great day this has been," he says. "A great day financially, a great day for John.... You have many friends, Senator."

Another passenger says he's disappointed, though, that the Hogg Junior High song hadn't been sung. So, with twin turbo-engines for accompaniment, Mr. Tower sings:

> *Hogg Junior High, Hogg Junior High,*
> *Where we're happy all the day,*
> *There's mirth and joy for every girl and boy,*
> *And all the teachers seem so happy and gay.*
> *We'll do our work, no one will shirk,*
> *We will hold your standards high. . . .*

John Tower had come home.

One night earlier in the summer, Penny Cook turned on the TV in the middle of *Saturday Night Live*. The cast was doing a spoof of *Cheers*. Sitting at the bar was an actor playing her father, John Tower.

"He was getting drunk and putting the move on women," Mrs.

Cook says. "I couldn't believe what I was seeing. I turned the TV off and said, 'Let it rest.' I know it was a rerun, but...."

Mrs. Cook's sister, Marian Tower, remembers the night David Letterman read his list of "John Tower's Top 10 Pickup Lines," and the night Jay Leno said her father "looks like Yoda with a bad haircut."

"Our family can laugh at just about anything," she says, "but that really hurt a lot. Just to be sitting and watching TV, trying to get your mind off of what was happening, and then to have the really, really tacky jokes thrown at you. The only time my father really lost his sense of humor about the situation was when the comedians started making jokes."

The "situation," of course, was the two-month-long hearings before the Senate Armed Services Committee about Mr. Tower's fitness to serve as President Bush's secretary of defense.

"The committee started out questioning my dad about issues of substance," Mrs. Cook says, "about things he would do in the Defense Department, about his beliefs on certain weapons systems. He answered their questions very well. The committee seemed real satisfied with his answers. We all felt things were fine. We came back to Texas thinking we would be returning to Washington in a week or two for his swearing-in."

But on Jan. 31, 1989, a conservative political activist named Paul Weyrich testified before the committee that he had seen Mr. Tower drunk and "with women to whom he is not married." Mr. Weyrich's testimony was never confirmed, but other informants came forward with similar claims. Then the FBI, which already had completed its background check on Mr. Tower, was ordered by Armed Services Committee Chairman Sam Nunn to do another. Soon it seemed that half the population of the country was claiming to have spotted Mr. Tower at one time or another swilling booze and chasing skirts from Washington to Geneva to Bergstrom Air Force Base and dallying with a non-existent Russian ballerina in Houston.

"It was bizarre," Mrs. Cook says. "It was a nightmare. The press would print something about a bad thing he was supposed to have done at a certain time at a certain place, and he would go through his calendar and show that he wasn't even at that place on that day, but that would never get printed. They would just go on to the next allegation. And each new rumor would feed another."

On March 9, when the Senate voted 53 to 47 not to confirm Mr. Tower, some who voted against him told the press they were worried that Mr. Tower might endanger national security by buddying up to defense contractors, drinking too much or pursuing women while in charge of the military forces. His defenders claimed the vote — which had been largely along partisan lines — had less to do with Mr. Tower's alleged moral lapses than with the desire of the Senate's Democratic majority to embarrass the new Republican president, and with Sen. Nunn's own presidential ambitions.

"I am inclined to question the use of raw FBI files and uncorroborated allegations, made in many instances by anonymous accusers," Mr. Tower says now, "and I am told by those who have reviewed the FBI files — I have not seen them — that the testimony of the people interviewed was overwhelmingly favorable."

Whatever the senators' motives had been for rejecting him, Mr. Tower decided to leave Washington. "No public figure in my memory," he said at the time, "has been subjected to such a far-reaching and thorough investigation nor had his human foibles bared to such intensive and demeaning public scrutiny. And yet there is no finding that I have ever breached established legal and ethical standards nor been derelict in my duty." It was his plan, he said, "to load up my 1972 Dodge Charger 400 Magnum with all my possessions, mattress strapped to the roof . . . and head back to Texas."

"John is a very *decent* man," says Dorothy Heyser, his friend who sat behind him in the hearing room day after day. "And when you're decent, and you know you've told the truth, and someone lies or twists your comments, what *can* you do? How *do* you fight it?"

The Senate's vote was a sharp blow to George Bush's new administration and a deep hurt to Mr. Tower's family and friends. "It was like a death after a long illness," says Martha Kirkendall, long-time manager of Mr. Tower's Dallas office.

Mr. Tower says it was simply politics. "That's Washington. It happens that way sometimes."

In 1988, John Tower reported to the Armed Services Committee that he earned $665,277 in consulting and director fees, most of it from defense firms, $74,000 for making speeches, $50,000 for lecturing to political science classes at Southern Methodist University, and $48,743 in federal pensions.

Last December, when President-elect Bush asked him to run the Pentagon, he canceled his consulting contracts, resigned his corporate directorships, disbanded his Dallas consulting firm, closed down his offices in Dallas and Washington, took a leave of absence from his position as distinguished lecturer at SMU and prepared to move to the Pentagon, where he would earn a salary of $99,500 a year, but control one-third of the trillion-dollar federal budget.

"There is no question this is the summit of his experiences, one that he was looking for all during his career," said Paul Eggers, Mr. Tower's longtime friend and Dallas business partner, when President Bush announced the appointment.

Indeed, during his years in the Senate, Mr. Tower had made national defense policy his special field of expertise. He rose to become the ranking minority member of the Armed Services Committee, and hoped a Ronald Reagan victory in the 1980 election might mean the defense secretariat for him. That hope was squelched, however, when the voters gave the Republicans a majority in the Senate, in addition to the White House. For the first time in Sen. Tower's 20-year tenure, his party was running things, and suddenly he was chairman of the Armed Services Committee and one of the most powerful men on Capitol Hill.

"It wouldn't have been practical to remove him from the chairmanship of such an important committee to make him secretary of defense," says Mrs. Kirkendall. "We found out later that Caspar Weinberger was Reagan's absolute, only choice for secretary of defense anyway. Nobody else was even considered. But Sen. Tower would have welcomed the opportunity, and we had a few weeks of uncertainty."

In 1984, Sen. Tower announced that he was "burned out" and would retire from the Senate the following year, at the end of his fourth term. He yearned for privacy and freedom, he says, but his return to private life kept getting postponed. Only two weeks after he left the Senate, Secretary of State George Shultz asked him to head the American side of the Strategic Arms Limitation Talks in Geneva, a post he held for 14 months. And only eight months after his resignation on April 1, 1986, President Reagan asked him to head the Iran-Contra review board that became popularly known as the Tower Commission.

He didn't enjoy the job, but the commission issued a tough report, criticizing the president for his lack of knowledge and control of the activities of Lt. Col. Oliver North and his associates, and recommending changes in the way the National Security Council had been operating. When he presented the report to President Reagan in February 1987, Mr. Tower was weary, emotionally drained and ready for a change of scene.

He returned to Dallas and formed a partnership with his old friend Paul Eggers and Timothy C. Greene, an attorney who formerly had been with the Securities and Exchange Commission and the Treasury Department. They incorporated the Tower, Eggers and Greene consulting firm with Mr. Tower as chairman.

The consulting work that the firm did for such defense companies as LTV, Martin-Marietta, Textron and Rockwell International — and which later would fuel the rumors in Washington that the defense secretary-designate was in the pocket of the defense contractors — provided the bulk of his income.

But he also had signed a contract with Cosby Bureau International, a Washington speakers' agency that handles such high-dollar banquet circuit riders as Dan Rather, Dr. Ruth Westheimer and Tommy Lasorda; had signed a contract with Little, Brown to write a scholarly study of the conflict between Congress and the White House over foreign policy; was team-teaching a course on foreign policy with Dr. James Brown of the SMU Political Science Department; and, after a British friend recommended him to Robert Maxwell, the flamboyant London press lord who was becoming a heavy player in the American publishing industry, Mr. Tower became chairman of Brassey's Defense Publications, a Maxwell-owned publisher of technical defense journals.

When Mr. Tower helped him acquire *Armed Forces Journal* in 1987, Mr. Maxwell named him chairman of that publication as well. And in November 1988, when Mr. Maxwell paid $2.7 billion for Macmillan, Inc., one of America's largest publishing houses, he placed Mr. Tower on its board.

Private life was treating Mr. Tower fine. Then he heeded the siren call of George Bush.

"When they asked John to accept that job, he gave up everything," says Mrs. Heyser. "And he was three months in Washington, living at his own expense, with no income. But he never complained about it. He said, 'Something will work out.' He couldn't have been more marvelous about it."

Senate Minority Leader Robert Dole described what happened to Mr. Tower as "an execution." Mr. Eggers said the Senate gave him "a scar he will carry the rest of his life." His daughter Marian thinks Mr. Eggers may be right. "This isn't something where you can say, 'Oh, he's over it,' she says. "I would guess that he has to wonder every day: 'Why did this happen?'"

Mr. Tower won't reveal his deeper feelings about the experience. "I'll reflect on it later on," he says. "I'm still reviewing what happened." But he has been assigned a special niche in American history — one he never wanted and never expected to occupy. In the 200 years that the Senate has been confirming the president's cabinet appointments, he's only the ninth to be rejected, and the first to be rejected in the first 90 days of a new president's administration.

"The Senate's vote," he says, "certainly brought to an end my full-time career as a public servant. The most difficult thing for me is turning away from the area that I've focused on for the last 20 years of my life. That, of course, is national security and foreign policy. But it's an adjustment I have to make."

He acknowledges that his reputation has been damaged, "but probably not as much as it appears on the surface. Many people have talked to me and written me letters — some liberal Democrats, even — expressing outrage over the way this thing was done.... There is an innate sense of fair play in the American people, and I think there is a general feeling that I was not fairly treated."

Mrs. Kirkendall, Mr. Eggers and his daughters all describe his reaction as "stoic" — so stoic, in fact, that Mrs. Cook worries about him. "I think he's the kind of person who might be more hurt than he would ever let on," she says. "He's going to hold his head up and go on, because that's the kind of person he is. But I think about him. I'm concerned. I don't want him to be sad."

Financially, Mr. Tower isn't without help in picking up the pieces. Almost immediately after the Senate vote, Robert Maxwell called from London, offering him back the board positions at Brassey's, the *Armed Forces Journal* and Maxwell-Macmillan. He accepted them. And although the pressures of the past two years had forced Mr. Tower to abandon work on his scholarly book on foreign policy, he has signed a new contract with Little, Brown for another book on the same subject. He's at work on it now with his collaborator, Washington free-lance writer Kathy Maxa.

"It's going to deal with the struggle between the Congress and the executive branch on national security and foreign policy matters," Mr. Tower says. "It'll go into congressional activism in the field, which pre-empts presidential prerogative or traditional authority in the area. But unlike the other book I was working on, it'll have a lot of anecdotal material in it. My own experience will be woven into the book, including the confirmation experience.

"In the post-World War II period, there was pretty much of a bipartisan approach to foreign policy — not just bipartisan in the sense of Republicans and Democrats, but bipartisan in the sense of legislative and executive. That began to deteriorate during the Vietnam War, and with the erosion of the seniority system and the loss of a sense of discipline in the Congress. The old saying was 'Politics ends at the water's edge.' And back in my early days, in the mid-'60s to the mid-'70s, I was rarely critical publicly of the administration's foreign policy, even under a Democratic administration. But that's all changed now. And it's a dangerous change for the country."

What should be done to correct it, he says, is "a long story, which we'll be writing." The book is going well, he says. "My collaborator is very diligent."

National security policy also is the topic of the speeches he makes to trade and professional associations, academic audiences and conclaves of corporate executives. Not long after the Senate vote, his agent, Joe Cosby, told a reporter that Mr. Tower was being paid $20,000 and up per appearance, but Mr. Tower says it isn't so. "My fee is pretty well fixed, and it's not that high," he says. "I don't want to discuss it ... I also do some pro bono speaking in addition to what I do or a fee."

And perhaps more important for the long run, the firm of Tower, Eggers and Greene has been reincorporated and is open for business again. This time, however, there will be no full-time consulting arrangements with defense companies. "I just don't feel like I want to go back to that," Mr. Tower says.

Mrs. Kirkendall, who has worked for Mr. Tower for 27 years, thinks the Senate hearings effected that decision. "He very strongly resisted any identity as a lobbyist," she says. "He never wanted to be a promoter on behalf of his clients and their interests with the government. He knew his role to be as an adviser. But his motives were impugned. And to go back to doing the same thing now, even though he would still have honorable motives, would just be read wrong."

The firm now, Mr. Tower says, is "largely in the business of marrying up investors with investment opportunities. And we're getting involved in some business opportunities that might give me a chance to gain some equity in something, instead of always working on a retainer basis."

One of the industries in which the firm is becoming involved is communications satellites, Mr. Eggers says, but neither he nor Mr. Tower will reveal more than that. "The company will have varied interests," Mr. Eggers says, "and John will now have something he's never had before — an interest in some assets that will make money for him, and someday for his children."

The only thing Mr. Tower hasn't recovered since his Senate ordeal is his lectureship at SMU. Almost immediately after Mr. Tower went to Washington to join the Bush administration, the university gave the lectureship to Bob Krueger, the former Democratic congressman who in 1978 almost ousted Mr. Tower from the Senate and may have contributed to his decision to retire. "Bob has the reputation of being a very fine teacher," Mr. Tower says.

Nevertheless, he plans still to lecture on foreign policy matters at SMU from time to time. And, since he's still a member of the president's Foreign Intelligence Advisory Board, which monitors the government's intelligence operations and makes recommendations to President Bush on how to improve them, he's not entirely exiled from the corridors of power in Washington.

"I still have many friends in government. I'm still socially acceptable in Washington," he says with a shadow of a smile. "And if some board or commission were created for some temporary purpose, something like the so-called Tower Commission, I might go back in that capacity. But for the time being — and for the foreseeable future — I'll be trying to build some business that will sustain me in my old age and give me something to pass on to my children. I want to help revive the economy of my state. I believe Texas and the Southwest are the wave of the future. Despite our recent travail over the decline of the price of crude, the decline in the value of commercial real estate and the accompanying decline of our financial institutions, Texas will come back."

In Austin, a reporter asks Mr. Tower how old he is.
"Sixty-three," he replies. "I don't look it, do I?"
He's joking, but the veteran pols talking about him in the corridor

aren't. "He's still young," one of them says. "I wouldn't be surprised if he ran again for something."

"How about governor?" his friend says. "In 1990?"

Mr. Tower smiles at the suggestion. "There's enough good candidate material in the Republican Party that we are in the happy position of not having to recall and retread older politicians," he says.

But he's home, and he intends to stay busy.

"Daddy isn't one to wallow in self-pity," says his daughter Marian. "He just wants to put it behind him and live on. He's very strong."

August 1989

A FAMILY NIGHTMARE

Of all the crimes of which a man can be accused, none is as slimy as sexual molestation of a child. So when one of my oldest friends sat across the table in a restaurant one morning and told me he had been accused of molesting his neighbor's little daughter... Of all the stories I've written during some 30 years of journalism, this one was the most difficult.

IN THE FRONT PEW OF THE COURTOOM, THE ACCUSER — BLOND, NOT quite four years old, pink ribbon in her hair, still clutching her doll and a bag of jelly beans — had fallen asleep in her father's lap. Beside them sat her mother and her grandmother and grandfather.

They had sat there nearly all the time since Judge Thomas Thorpe turned the case over to the jury at 11:07 a.m. on the fifth day of the trial, a Friday. Except for the intermittent comings and goings of bailiffs and clerks and lawyers concerned with other cases in the judge's court, the family was alone in the courtroom. From time to time, one of the adults would turn to another and say something in a low voice, but most of the time they were silent, gazing into the middle distance like parishioners who had arrived too early for a church service.

Just outside the courtroom, on a bench beside the door, the accused — slightly balding, just turned 40, wearing a suit that his wife had bought at a garage sale and a tie he had borrowed from his lawyer — was sleeping, too, sitting upright, tie still straight, coat still buttoned neatly.

About him buzzed the voices of a dozen or more relatives and friends — some from distant cities who had come to Dallas at their own expense to testify to his good character and reputation, some from his neighborhood who had taken off from work to be with his wife, Michele, and his mother, Thelma, when the verdict came in. Just under the surface of their casual words lay a dull edge of fear.

About 4 p.m., April 27, 1990, five hours after the jury had retired to reach its verdict, Darryl Hughes, a private detective who worked for the defense attorney, turned to me and whispered what nobody else in the corridor had dared say: "I don't like this. I'm getting a real bad feeling."

On the afternoon of June 20, 1989, the day his nightmare would begin, James took his mother, who was visiting from out of town, to see the Sixth Floor, the exhibit about the assassination of John F. Kennedy. While they were gone, a stranger came to the house in North Oak Cliff where James and Michele live and work.

Michele, who was nursing her infant son when the stranger knocked, handed the child to the babysitter and answered the door. The stranger identified herself as Alice Umbach, a caseworker for the Texas Department of Human Services. She asked to talk to Michele in private. When they were alone, Ms. Umbach said: "Your husband has been charged with sexually molesting your neighbors' daughter, Sally."

Sally is the three-year-old girl next door, the adopted daughter of Stephanie and Fred. Sally had been a frequent playmate of Michele and James' own four-year-old, Clara.

Ms. Umbach said Stephanie believed James had molested Clara, as well as Sally.

"That's not possible!" Michele said. "My husband would never do anything like that!"

"Where is your daughter?" Ms. Umbach asked.

Michele told her Clara was playing down the street.

"Well, I have to get a statement from her," Ms. Umbach said, "or else I'm going to have to take her with me or have your husband leave the house."

"She was real brusque," Michele remembers. "She reminded me of, like, a bill collector."

Michele agreed to go to the house where Clara was playing and bring her home. Ms. Umbach insisted on accompanying her. "At that time," Ms. Umbach's report reads, "the mother seemed very, very upset, but more shocked than anything."

They returned with the little girl, and, to be out of earshot of the babysitter in the house, they went to the second floor of the garage, where Michele and James — both of whom are professional artists — have separate studios.

"She talked to Clara in my studio," Michele remembers, "and I went into James' studio. I closed the door. I couldn't hear what she was saying. I was so upset I could hardly catch my breath."

Ms. Umbach reports it differently: "She was hovering very closely by, and kept walking by and poking her head into the room. I explained to Michele once again that I needed to talk to her daughter alone, but she seemed very hesitant to do so. It was very difficult to keep Clara's attention while Michele kept walking back and forth.

"Clara . . . seemed very fascinated with my purse. We started going through different items in my purse and me telling her what they were. . . . Every time I would try to get to the sexual abuse, she would quit talking, say she did not want to talk, or put her head down. I told her that I knew it was very difficult for her to talk about this, but that it was my job to talk to little girls like her and find out about these things so they wouldn't happen anymore. She still refused to discuss it."

Michele, believing the caseworker was badgering her child, came back into the room. Ms. Umbach's report says, "I told her that Sally had already told the police and a child psychologist about the abuse, and although I had not had a chance to interview her myself, I felt very strongly that the child's statements were accurate.

"I then started to try to talk to Clara again," the report says, "and Michele stated, 'Go ahead, tell her that nobody has touched you like that.' I then decided that this was not going to work.... I told Michele that I realized she was very upset, but that she was hampering my investigation by insisting on being very nearby when I interviewed her child."

At that point, James came up the stairs. He saw Michele's face and said, "What's wrong?"

Michele introduced him to Ms. Umbach. "Can you step in here?" Ms. Umbach asked. The four of them — including Clara — went into Michele's studio. Ms. Umbach shut the door. "You've been charged with sexually molesting your neighbors' daughter, Sally," she told James.

"What?" James said. "Is this some kind of bad joke? I'll take a polygraph test!"

Ms. Umbach told James the crime against Sally had taken place in Clara's bedroom, with her also present, while Michele was taking a nap. "You put your finger in her vagina," she said. "It was digital penetration."

"She stated it like it was a fact," James said later. "In a real intimidating kind of tone, a bullying kind of attitude. And Clara was standing there in shock."

According to Michele, Ms. Umbach then looked and her and said, "I still need to get a statement from your daughter, or I am taking her with me. Maybe you can help me."

The two women and Clara returned to James' studio. Michele took her daughter into her lap. Ms. Umbach asked Clara: "Has your papa ever touched you where you go tee-tee?"

"No," Clara said. She laid her head on her mother's shoulder.

"Has your papa ever touched Sally where she goes tee-tee?" Ms. Umbach asked.

The child hid her face in Michele's shoulder. Then she got up and walked about the room, then came back to her mother's lap.

Michele repeated Ms. Umbach's question. "I asked her a couple more times, and so did Umbach," Michele said later. "Finally, when I asked her again if Papa had touched Sally, she shook her head. No."

Ms. Umbach told Michele that, based on her daughter's responses to the questions, she believed Clara had been sexually molested.

Michele asked Ms. Umbach if she and James should get a lawyer. Ms. Umbach reports: "I told them that was up to them."

But Michele remembers the response differently: "She told me, 'You don't need to call a lawyer. This might be nothing. I haven't talked to Stephanie, and I haven't talked to Sally, so you don't need to get a lawyer.'"

Ms. Umbach's report indicates she and Stephanie had talked on the phone earlier in the day. It was their first contact. Ms. Umbach hadn't yet talked with Sally, and wouldn't for another week.

Michele recalls the caseworker's final comments as she was leaving: "I'm sorry, Michele. Women have this happen. I know it's really a shock for you. But you need to protect your children." She said Michele would have to bring Clara to the DHS office later for an extended interview.

"I went back into the house," Michele said. "James was sitting in the chair in our bedroom, looking like he had been hit by a train."

Together, they walked back to their studios, and Michele called a lawyer. He told her to come with James to his office immediately.

At 9:30 that evening, Michele walked over and knocked on her neighbor's door. Stephanie opened it. "Just a minute," she said. "I'm on the phone." She returned to the phone. "Michele is here," she said, and hung up.

"Oh, Michele," she said as she returned. "I never meant to hurt you."

"James and I feel like we've been hit in the face with a baseball bat," Michele said.

"Michele, it happened, and it's true, and it has happened many times," Stephanie said.

"I told her that I didn't believe James would ever do that," Michele said later. "But judging from her face I could tell she truly believed James would do such a thing. I tried to stay calm, and asked her when this was supposed to have happened. She said it had been happening for over a year! And she told me that Sally had had recurring yeast infections way back since September. I told Stephanie that I had been sexually abused by my grandfather when I was a child, and how I had just gone through an incest recovery program, mostly because of James' love and support. And that if Sally was abused, I knew how she might feel, and I could imagine how Stephanie would feel.

"I told her that our friendship was important, and that Sally was important to us, but to please really think and be sure before she pointed the finger at James."

James and I have been friends for a long time. We worked together for several years, and after he quit the magazine where I worked and became a free-lance illustrator we would meet for lunch from time to time to catch up on each other's lives. So I wasn't surprised to come to work and find a phone message from him: "Must meet you for coffee immediately. Emergency." It was typical of his messages when he wants to get away from the drawing board for a while. I called him, and we arranged to meet at a restaurant in Oak Cliff.

As we sat down, I noticed that his face was a pale gray, as if he had been ill for a long time, but I didn't remark on it. We sipped our coffee and made the usual small talk for a few minutes, then he quietly dropped the bomb: "A woman came to my house and accused me of sexually molesting my next-door neighbors' little girl."

I was speechless. How does a man respond to such a statement? Of all the crimes and sins that can be attached to a man's name, sexual molestation of a child is the filthiest and most unmanly.

"I would rather be accused of murder," James said. He was speaking calmly, unemotionally, as he always does, but his eyes were full of anger and fear.

He told of Alice Umbach's visit the day before, and his and Michele's meeting a few hours late with Gary Noble, the lawyer Michele had called. Mr. Noble had been recommended to her, James said, by the director of the Incest Recovery Association, where Michele recently had undergone group therapy.

"Noble says this is what they call a 'super felony,'" James said. "If I'm convicted, I could go to prison for five years to life. There's no probation, unless the jury gives it. The judge can't give probation in a super felony case."

I was remembering stories I had heard about the treatment that child molesters receive from their fellow inmates. I was trying to imagine what the lives of Michele and the children would be if James went to prison.

Then James asked if I would write about his case.

"Follow me through it," he said. "From the inside."

"Why would you want that?" I asked.

"So I won't get swallowed up by the system without somebody knowing about it," he said.

Two days after Alice Umbach's visit, Gary Noble had arranged for James to take a polygraph test with Wayne Baker, a private investigator who specializes in the field. James told me the Dallas police had assigned his case to the Youth and Family Crime Division. "I could get arrested, get handcuffed and taken to jail at any time," he said.

James asked Mr. Baker if I could sit in on the test. The investigator said that would breach the confidentiality that he liked to keep with his clients, but that James could show me the results later, if he wished.

He grilled James for three hours, asking all sorts of questions, but always leading back to *the* question, which he asked in three slightly different ways: "Did you put your finger in the vagina of Sally?"

"No," James replied each time. After the session, James showed me the polygrapher's report. He had passed.

Two days after that, a Saturday morning, Mr. Noble had James call together his neighbors to tell them of the accusation.

It's a typical middle-class North Oak Cliff block, lined with old trees and close-together, 60-year-old brick houses. Most of the older residents have sold their homes in recent years to couples now in their 30s and early 40s, most of them with a small child or two.

The couples have repaired the houses and settled down to raise their babies in the quiet, humdrum way that people of their generation imagine the ideal American family life to be. Many of them, because of their common interest in parenthood, have become close friends. They have dinner in each other's homes, pool their junk for yard sales, borrow each other's tools, babysit each other's children. On the witness stand, James would call it "a *Leave It to Beaver* kind of neighborhood."

One couple who didn't participate in neighborhood activities were Stephanie and Fred. The only people on the block that they hobnobbed with were James and Michele, and Clara was Sally's only regular playmate on the street. "We don't socialize much," Stephanie would testify during the trial.

James wasn't yet prepared to tell his mother, Thelma, who was still visiting, of the accusation, so his neighborhood friends — about a dozen of them — convened at another house. James and Michele already had told them of Alice Umbach's visit. The men, especially, were worried about the accusation against James. "It makes you aware of your vulnerability," one of them said. "This could happen to anybody."

"My knees buckled when I heard about it," said another. "I was in shock."

"I feel like I've got a rock about the size of a cantaloupe in my stomach," James said. He told them that Sally had been taken to a psychologist who put her through play therapy with anatomically explicit dolls — a Mama doll, a Daddy doll, a Michele doll and a Papa doll. (Sally, like his own daughter, called James "Papa.") "And she kept saying it was the Papa doll who put his finger inside her," James said. "I've helped potty train her, and changed her diaper. I've treated her just like my own daughter. . . . "

"Stephanie and I would go off to garage sales," Michele said, "and the guys would take turns taking care of the kids. . . . "

"The opportunity was there," James said.

Gary Noble arrived and was introduced to the neighbors. He told them of Ms. Umbach's visit again, and the seriousness of the charge against James. "So the system marches on. The system hasn't even talked to Sally yet, but the system already has concluded that James is guilty of a first-degree felony called aggravated sexual assault. . . .

"There are children out there who get molested," he said. "There's no question about that. For years nobody did anything about it. Now all of a sudden *everybody* is doing *everything* about it. There are people called 'true believers' who believe that one out of four children are molested. They believe that children always tell the truth and that children can't be coached. If these people had their way — and thank God they don't — James would be in jail until he admitted he did it, and then he would go to treatment and get some help, and then he would go to the penitentiary. This is like the Salem witch trials, where people were put to death for what a 10- or 11-year-old girl said."

He told them about the lie-detector test: "When I called Wayne Baker yesterday, he said, 'Your man is on the right side. He's telling the truth.'"

He told them that Ms. Umbach or another DHS worker might come around the neighborhood wanting to talk to their own children. "If you are harassed or threatened," he told them, "call a lawyer. But not me."

"We're living in a touchless society," Mr. Noble said. "Every time I change my own kid's diaper, I think of that."

Although the police hadn't yet contacted James, Mr. Noble already was preparing his defense. A week after the neighbors' meeting, he sent James to Dr. Robert Powitzky, a psychologist, to take a battery of tests. The tests were designed to determine whether James fit the profile of a sex offender. During a second session the next day, a sensor was attached to his penis and to a computer, and he was shown slides of naked women and children.

"It was humiliating," James said later. "Some of the kids were prepubescent, some looked like they had just entered puberty, and some were real little kids — three, four, five years old. They were really awful slides, awful photography, real amateurish. I kept thinking, 'My God, these are the actual slides they've confiscated from real perverts.' They made me physically ill. I thought I was going to throw up a few times."

Then Dr. Powitzky questioned him for two hours. "About two-thirds of the way through the interview," James said, "I think it was obvious to him that I wasn't guilty. He told me that if the woman from Human Services called again, Michele should say to her, 'I'm taking all steps necessary to ensure that my kids are safe.' He said she should imply a little glimmer of doubt about my innocence, because if they believe Michele is protecting me or is leaving the kids alone with me, they'll take the kids away from us or, at the very least, make me move out of the house."

While James was being tested, all the neighbors who had been at the Saturday meeting with Gary Noble had sent their children to James and Michele's house to play with Clara. "It was gratifying," James said later. But since Alice Umbach's visit, Clara had become "real clingy," he said. "A couple of times a day, she'll tell both of us that she loves us. She's more lovey-dovey than usual."

Meanwhile, Gary Noble had persuaded Ms. Umbach's supervisor, Lynne Johnson, to allow Clara to be interviewed by Brenda Keller, an independent psychologist, rather than by Ms. Umbach or a psychologist affiliated with the Department of Human Services. Ms. Keller had worked for the DHS for 15 years before going into private practice.

Ms. Keller was to have a few get-acquainted sessions with Clara, win her confidence, then try to find out if she had been sexually molested, or if she had seen Sally being molested, as Stephanie claimed. A videotape was to be made of the interview.

On July 6 Michele and Clara returned home from what was supposed to have been the videotape session. Michele was tired and discouraged. Clara had refused to talk about Sally.

"As soon as Brenda mentioned Sally, Clara just clammed up," Michele said. "Alice Umbach had scared her out of her wits. Whenever Brenda mentioned Sally, Clara just climbed on my lap and wouldn't talk.

"Then Brenda told me I had to be careful about leaving James around Clara," Michele said. "And I told her, 'I've been married to this man for seven years. He's the most honest man I've ever met. With my history with my grandfather, I would pick up on something like that. He's never given me the slightest hint of ever being that way. He's a wonderful father.' And she said that for my protection I had to make sure Clara is never alone with James. She said, 'You have to think the worst.'"

Michele was near tears. "Clara has always been a shy child," she said. "She never has warmed up to strangers easily. And they're misinterpreting her personality and using it against us.

"I feel like this whole thing is to trap us," she said. "It's like they're trying to trap us into admitting that something happened that didn't, like they're trying to break up our family."

Michele had told Ms. Keller that her gynecologist had examined Clara a few days earlier and had found no evidence of sexual abuse. "That doesn't mean anything," Ms. Keller had replied. "He could have partial penetration. He could put his tongue on her. He could fondle her."

"Nothing we do means anything," James said. "I'm getting tired of being the target. I feel like turning around and going on the offensive. I'm tired of just sitting around waiting for things to happen to me."

While James and Michele were worrying about Clara's refusal to talk to Ms. Keller, Alice Umbach's attempt to videotape Sally's accusation was failing, too. "For some reason, the minute that we walked into the videotape room, Sally was terrified," her report says. "She did not like the dolls, she did not like the room, but I went ahead and convinced her to stay. As I started the tape . . . when we started about the abuse, she all of a sudden got up, cried, asked for her mother and literally ran out of the room."

They returned to Ms. Umbach's office, and, with Stephanie present, Sally told of being touched by a man and told of a man masturbating in her presence. She said Clara also was present, and that the man was James. Ms. Umbach didn't insist on talking with the child alone, as she had with Clara.

Carol Gregston, a detective with the Youth and Family Crime Division of the Dallas Police Department, joined them, and the child repeated her accusation for her.

"Carol seemed quite reluctant to file on this case, saying Sally is a very poor witness," Ms. Umbach's report says. "I told Carol that I felt there was sufficient evidence to at least go ahead and refer it to the grand jury. Stephanie felt the same way. I told Carol that I did not want to wait to see if there was any physical evidence. . . .

"Carol then started talking about waiting for a couple of years before they filed the case, waiting for the child to be older so she could testify better. Stephanie stated that she did not want her child to have to go through this in a couple of years. I also reminded Carol that we were going to have the child in play therapy and that she would be a lot better witness by the time the case came up. The reason Carol had a problem with this was because she felt the witness had to be led a little bit. She could not basically just say, 'What has happened between you and James and Clara?'"

In late July, Dr. Powitzky asked James to return to his office for a consultation. He allowed James to tape-record their conversation. Dr. Powitzky confronted him with the stories that Sally had told to Ms. Umbach and that Ms. Umbach had passed on to Ms. Keller.

James again denied that he had ever touched Sally, except when he had to clean her up after she dirtied her pants while playing at his house — an accident that had happened frequently during the months Stephanie was potty-training her.

"One time I had to put her in the bathtub, she was so bad," James said. "Once I hosed her off with a garden hose outside. I had to wash her clothes and let her have some of Clara's."

As he was concluding the consultation, Dr. Powitzky said: "It's going to be an uphill fight for you. Apparently she's a very verbal little girl. . . . I'll just be real blunt with you. Sometimes we've worked with guys, I never would have thought they had done anything, and then finally they'll just come out and say, 'Yeah, I didn't do that, but I did do this. . . .'

"If that were your case, which you're saying it's not, I just wanted to give you a chance, because obviously your wife and your daughter are going to go through a lot more rough time. If you did do something and you're denying it, it's going to be rougher on them than if you did do something and you admit that you did something."

James, barely containing his anger, replied: "I have never had a sexual thought about a child in my entire life. Period."

"Got it," Dr. Powitzky said.

By Aug. 10, seven weeks into his ordeal, James thought it was about to end. A physician finally had examined Sally and found no physical evidence of sexual abuse. Once the police got around to interviewing him, James thought, the case would be dropped. "When the police get involved, they're not going to look just at me," he said, "they're going to look at all sides of it. There's no evidence against me except the statement of this little kid. And my lawyer thinks they'll look at that and say, 'Is this all there is? We're not going to make fools of ourselves for something like this.'"

James and Michele had begun to plan a vacation with her family in Michigan in September. "After my interview with the police, I feel like we can go without looking like we're trying to run away," James said.

But the police didn't show up. Not long after her meeting on June 28 with Alice Umbach and Stephanie and Sally, Detective Gregston had gone on vacation, and when she returned, she was assigned temporarily to other duty. She never went to James' house, and never interviewed Clara, who — according to Stephanie and Sally — was a witness to a felony and also a victim. She never questioned anyone in James' neighborhood. Her entire investigation consisted of three conversations with Sally.

She told me later that she had been hampered by the fact that Clara was seeing Brenda Keller instead of a DHS psychologist, and by the fact that James had a lawyer. "He had a right to do what he did," Detective Gregston said, "to contact an attorney the moment he was notified that an investigation was under way."

Meanwhile, Detective Gregston and her sergeant were getting phone calls from Stephanie and Alice Umbach, pressuring them to take the case to the grand jury. Neither the detective's reluctance nor the physician's failure to find evidence that Sally had been molested had shaken their resolve. "Although Stephanie seemed very disappointed (with the doctor's report), I told her that I still felt Detective Gregston would go ahead and file against James . . . for indecency with a child," Ms. Umbach's report said.

Two months after James was accused, Detective Gregston finally called him and asked him to come to police headquarters for questioning. James referred her to his attorney. The detective then called Gary Noble and asked him to bring his client in for a polygraph.

"He has already taken a polygraph," Mr. Noble replied. "It clearly shows he's telling the truth."

Detective Gregston said she still wanted to talk to James, "to get his side of it."

"I can tell you his side of it," Mr. Noble said. "He didn't do it."

Mr. Noble finally agreed to bring James in, and he made an appointment. Later, he changed his mind. "We had nothing to say to her," he said, "except that James didn't do it." He decided not to keep the appointment, but he failed to inform Detective Gregston. And, Detective Gregston said later, he didn't return her phone calls. So she went before the Dallas County grand jury and recommended that James be indicted for aggravated sexual assault.

He was.

About 11 a.m. on Sept. 7 James was working in his studio. He heard a whistle and looked out the window. A uniformed police officer was standing in his back yard. "Are you the owner of this house?" the officer asked.

"Yeah," James said.

"Come out front and talk to me a minute."

James walked through his house and opened the front door. Four policemen were standing on the front porch. One of them called James by his name.

"Yes?"

"You have been indicted by the grand jury. We have a warrant for your arrest."

The officers handcuffed and frisked James and put him into the back seat of a police car. As they were about to haul him away, Michele and a friend arrived home from a shopping trip.

"Stephanie had taken off from work and had come home and set up a camera on a tripod and was videotaping James' arrest from her front door," Michele told me a few minutes later. She was crying. "This just drives me crazy," she said. "It's so humiliating. The whole thing is so disgusting. I'm just glad Clara is in school and wasn't here to see it. She wouldn't have been able to understand. She has been affected by this much too much already."

James was released 13 hours later on $10,000 bond.

The indictment read at the arraignment in Judge Thomas Thorpe's 203rd District Court on Sept. 20 said that "on or about the first day of November 1988," James "did then and there knowingly and intentionally cause the penetration of the sexual organ, namely the vagina of Sally, a child, by the finger of said defendant, and, at the time of this offense, the said child was younger than 14 years of age."

"How do you plead? Guilty or not guilty?" Judge Thorpe asked.

"Not guilty," James replied.

His trial was scheduled to begin Sept. 27, but the judge, Mr. Noble and Assistant District Attorney Faith Johnson, who was prosecuting the case, agreed to postpone it until Oct. 20.

After the hearing, Michele told me she was worried about her father, who had loaned them the money to hire Gary Noble. "He's taking this hard," she said. "He's very upset and very angry. His heart has been giving him a lot of trouble."

A few days later, Michele received a call that her father had had a heart attack at his home in Michigan. Later that same day, James' stepsister called to tell him that his father, who had been ill for a long time, had died in North Carolina.

As James was returning home from his father's funeral, he met Michele and the children at D/FW Airport, where they were getting on a plane to Michigan to visit Michele's father.

On Oct. 17, when Michele had been gone about two weeks, James' bail bondsman called him. The man was angry. "You missed your trial date," he said. "Now they've forfeited your bond. They'll issue a warrant for your arrest."

Terrified, James tried to call Gary Noble. He was in the midst of a trial in Denton.

Later that day, Mr. Noble learned that a slip of paper stating that James' trial date had been changed from Sept. 27 to Oct. 20 either hadn't been placed in the court's file folder as it should have been, or it had been lost. Neither the defense nor the prosecution showed up in Judge Thorpe's courtroom on Sept. 27, but as far as the judge was concerned, James was a fugitive from justice.

Mr. Noble advised his client to stay away from his home, in case an arrest warrant had been issued and the police were looking for him. James spent an uneasy night at my house.

When the snafu was straightened out, he went before Judge Thorpe again. The judge was still fuming. "I guess you realize that if you are convicted of this you could get life in prison as a maximum punishment," he said.

"Yes, sir," James said.

"How do you plead to this, guilty or . . . "

"Not guilty!" James shouted.

But James still wasn't close to his day in court. Faith Johnson had decided to run for district judge on the Republican ticket and had passed the case on to another prosecutor, Lynn Carsunis. Ms. Carsunis asked the judge to postpone the trial again so that Sally could have minor surgery for a recurring throat problem. Judge Thorpe, whose office was in chaos anyway because Dallas County's criminal courts were in the midst of a move from the courthouse to the new Frank Crowley Courts Building, reset the trial for Dec. 11.

Michele and James began thinking everything would be resolved by Christmas.

Then, in late November, the judge decided to hold a hearing to determine Sally's competency as a witness. He set the hearing for Jan. 12 and reset the trial for Jan. 29, 1990.

In January, however, Sally underwent throat surgery again. The competency hearing wouldn't be held until March 28.

"Meanwhile, Sally is getting older and older, which makes her a better witness," Mr. Noble said. "She was two years old when the abuse allegedly happened, and she'll be almost four when she testifies. I'm convinced she's being coached. I'm sure they're rehearsing her very thoroughly."

James' anger was collapsing into resignation. "What happens happens," he said. "There's nothing I can do about it. It's the way the system works. I'm sure the DA's office thinks, 'Well, let's see if he'll crack. Let's see if he'll run out of money.' But I'm a patient man."

When the day for the competency hearing finally rolled around, Lynn Carsunis was no longer prosecuting the case. She had resigned to become the director of the proposed Dallas Children's Advocacy Center and had been replaced by Patrick Kirlin.

As the hearing began, the judge came down from the bench and sat near the table where Sally sat with her mother. Both of Sally's grandfathers and one of her grandmothers were there, but her father, Fred, wasn't.

"Let me give her an oath . . ." the judge said. "Sally, I'm the judge, and I'm going to listen to what you have to say. But I want you to make me a promise. Will you?"

Sally nodded.

"You know what I want you to promise me?"

"What?"

"That you will tell me the truth, just exactly what happened."

"OK," Sally said.

"Will you promise me that?"

Sally nodded.

Mr. Kirlin asked her questions about herself, her parents and her grandparents. He asked her to name her favorite colors, to count to 10, to tell him about her trip to Disneyland. "If I told you that there was a big elephant sitting in that chair," he said, "would I be telling you the truth or would I be telling you a lie?"

"Lie," she said.

"Why is that?"

"Because elephants don't sit in chairs."

"Is there one over there right now?"

"No."

"OK. Good girl."

Gary Noble then asked Sally about her day care center, her favorite story, her favorite food, about toys, about Christmas gifts: "What did you get?"

"Butterflies."

"Butterflies? Real butterflies?"

"Yeah."

"Boy. How many?"

Sally held up her hand as if counting on her fingers.

"Five butterflies?" Mr. Noble said. "Six butterflies? Ten butterflies?"

"Yeah."

Then suddenly Mr. Noble asked, "Did James do anything to you?"

"No," Sally replied.

"What are you going to do after you get out of here?" Mr. Noble asked.

"I'm going to get some chips," Sally said.

Mr. Noble asked her several questions about potato chips, then said: "Are you afraid of James?"

"Yes," she replied.

"You are? Did James do something to you?"

"No."

He asked her about James and Michele, and about Clara. "They also have a little boy, don't they?" he said.

"No."

"They don't?"

"No."

"A little younger boy?"

"No."

He asked her about Mickey Mouse and Pluto and Daffy Duck and Bugs Bunny. Then he asked: "Did Clara do something to you?"

"No," Sally said.

"Did Stephanie do something to you?"

"No."

"Did Michele do something to you?"

"No."

"Did somebody do something to you?"

Sally looked at her mother. "Yes," she said.

"Who?"

"James."

"What did he do?"

"Don't know."

"You don't?" Mr Noble said. "Do you mean by that you don't know or you don't want to tell?"

"Don't want to tell."

"When James did something to you," he said, "who was there?"

"No one," Sally replied.

If Judge Thorpe should decide Sally was incompetent to testify against James, the DA's case would collapse and there would be no trial. But by April 5, he still hadn't issued a ruling.

"I'm drained of all my energy," James said. "All I've been doing is taking naps and sitting by the phone."

Later that day, Michele called me. "We're going to trial," she said. "The judge ruled her competent. Can you believe this? Is this real?"

James, on the other hand, suddenly was exhilarated. "I had almost made up my mind to *insist* on a trial if it had been dropped," he said. "I don't know if I actually would have gone through with it or not, but I like to think I might have. I'm so angry that I *want* to fight. I want to get into an arena where at last the truth will come out and I can have my say."

Judge Thorpe set the trial for April 24. A few days before it was to begin, Mr. Noble learned that Fred wasn't planning to attend, that he would be out of town on business. Mr. Noble subpoenaed him.

Darryl Hughes, the private investigator, took the subpoena to Fred's house and knocked on the door.

Fred answered. Sally was with him. Mr. Hughes handed Fred the subpoena. "Hello, Sally," he said.

Sally smiled. "Hi."

"How do you know my daughter?" Fred asked.

"I'm a detective," Mr. Hughes said.

Stephanie was the first witness. "I considered us very close friends," she said. "Our children played together daily. There was not a day that went by that they weren't at each other's houses. . . . Sometimes as many as four times a week, we would share meals together." Sometimes she and Michele would drive to garage sales together, she said. Sometimes Fred would watch the children while they were gone, and sometimes James would.

Then one day, she said, she was drying off Sally after her bath, and Sally "asked me to put my finger in her. I said to her that we don't do that to other people. She said, 'Yes, we do.' I said, 'No, we don't,' and she said, 'Yes.' I said, 'Has someone done that to you?' and she said, 'Yes.'"

Stephanie asked her if Clara had done it. Sally said she didn't. "I asked her if Michele had done it," Stephanie said, "and she said, 'No.' I asked her if her daddy had done it, and she said, 'No.' I asked her if James did it and she said, 'Yes.'"

Stephanie said Sally calls her vagina her "tushy." She said Sally told her James touched her tushy during "parties" in his studio, where she and Clara were "finger painting and eating oranges." Stephanie said she thought the molestation had occurred "on or about Nov. 1" because she remembered that the weather was cool when she went to pick up Sally and the child told her about the oranges and finger painting.

Sally followed her mother to the witness stand. She was self-possessed and cute and blond. When she sat down, only the top of her head and her eyes could be seen above the wall surrounding the witness stand. The six women on the jury leaned forward and smiled maternally at her.

"Do you remember back when you and Clara and James had parties in the studio?" Mr. Kirlin asked her.

"Uh-huh," Sally said.

"Can you tell me what happened at the parties?"

"I don't remember."

"Do you remember something that James did to you?"

"Yes."

"Can you tell me what that was?"

"He touched my tushy."

"Do you remember where that happened?"
"Uh-huh."
"And where was that?"
"In the bathroom."
"Do you remember where else it happened?"
"No."

Mr. Kirlin never called Clara, the alleged eyewitness, to testify, nor did he call the physician who examined Sally, nor introduce the physician's report into evidence. But many witnesses would follow Sally to the stand.

Detective Gregston would try to defend her investigation of the case from Gary Noble's withering ridicule. "Do you mean to tell me you had a walking, talking, living, breathing eyewitness and never tried to talk to her?" he asked when she admitted she had never questioned Clara. "Do you mean to tell me you never warned the parents of the other kids on the block that there was a child molester in the neighborhood?"

Mr. Noble began his defense with Mary Frances Gassett, a schoolteacher who lives across the street from Stephanie and Fred. Mrs. Gassett testified that Stephanie approached her one morning last July and said: "I hate to tell you this, but James has been molesting Sally and Clara for over a year now."

Mrs. Gassett said she replied: "You ought to be more careful before you go around accusing people of things like that."

She said that Sally, who was with her mother, chimed in: "But Mom, Papa (her name for James) didn't touch my pee-pee."

She said Stephanie picked up Sally and hurried back across the street.

During the five days of testimony, Michele would tell of Alice Umbach's visit and of James' goodness as a husband and father.

James would present a detailed calendar of his life from April 1988, when Stephanie and Fred had moved in next door, until Ms. Umbach's visit in June 1989, showing he had little opportunity for the regular abuse that Stephanie alleged. He would describe his household's daily routine, and his babysitting with Sally and Clara, and his cleaning-up of Sally's potty-training accidents. He would testify that there had never been any "parties" or finger painting in the studios.

Twenty-two neighbors and friends of James — many had traveled from as far away as California, Georgia, Tennessee and Ohio — would testify to his good character and reputation, and to his devotion as a husband and father.

Julie Ogg, a lifelong friend of Michele's, would tell of a bizarre episode she said she had witnessed in which Fred came to Michele's house to get his daughter. Sally became hysterical and tried to hide from him, Mrs. Ogg said, and Fred threatened to "take her back to the orphanage." The child then stopped crying, Mrs. Ogg said.

Fred would testify that the episode never happened, and that he hardly ever kept the children when Stephanie and Michele were away, but that James did.

Alice Umbach would deny that she had been rude or abusive during her visit to James' family.

Stephanie's other next-door neighbor, Kathleen Maloney, would testify that she hadn't rallied to James' side as the other neighbors did after he was accused. She had had her locks changed instead.

But the crux of the case was simple: Would the jurors believe, beyond a reasonable doubt, that Sally was a reliable witness and what she had told them was the truth?

Sally was the only evidence in the case, Mr. Noble argued, and she had been coached for nearly a year by Stephanie and the Department of Human Services.

Sally was telling the truth, Mr. Kirlin argued, and James was "an artist, a master of deception."

Sally was in the courtroom, sitting on Fred's lap, clutching her doll, while the lawyers made their arguments. The women on the jury kept looking at her.

At 11:07 a.m. Judge Thorpe turned the case over to the jurors, and they left the courtroom. Mr. Noble stalked into the hallway and exploded. "In all the years I've been practicing law, I've never seen a three-year-old alleged victim sitting in the courtroom during the arguments!" he said. "That may be a first in the United States!"

At 6:04 p.m. the red light beside the witness box finally flashed on. The jury had reached its verdict. James' friends streamed into the courtroom. "Bring in the jury," Judge Thorpe said. An awful tension fell upon the room.

"We, the jury, find the defendant not guilty," the presiding juror said.

Suddenly Fred and Stephanie and Sally and the grandparents were gone, and the women in the audience were weeping. Michele was weeping. Gary Noble was weeping. James rose from his chair at the defendant's table and numbly accepted the embraces of his friends. Darryl Hughes, who had had the bad feeling, whooped with joy. Everybody applauded.

"My daughter was in therapy for at least six months, and she went through hell before that," Stephanie told me over the phone. "She started wetting her bed and has not been able to get past that, and that's a real hard stigma now that she's four. We went through night after night of nightmares and yelling in the middle of the night over this. . . . Listen, from my perspective, James did this. There is no doubt in my mind that he did this. Absolutely none."

"Will you and your family continue to live next door to James and Michele?" I asked. "That must be difficult for all of you."

"The difficulty for us is not living next door to them" she said. "The pain for us is how the neighborhood reacted to this. But no, we're not moving. It's our home. We chose to live there. I'm not going to be run out of the neighborhood."

A few days after the trial, Michele saw Fred out in his yard and called to him: "There's the liar."

He responded, "Michele, you told a few yourself."

She said, "Fred, I didn't lie."

Another day, a limb fell off one of James' trees into Fred's yard. Fred tossed it into James' yard. They tossed it back and forth for about four days. Although Fred wasn't in sight, James exploded: "Next time I see this limb in my yard I'm going to stick it . . ."

"If he had come out of the house at that moment," James told me, "I think I would have murdered him. All the anger of the last 10 months came back at that moment."

Including work they lost because of the time they had to spend on the case, James and Michele estimate it cost them between $50,000 and $60,000 — much of it borrowed. "And a lot of emotional damage has been done to us," Michele said. "It's going to take a lot of time to recover. It's so horrible to have somebody you thought was your friend do this to you. And they still believe . . . "

One day they looked out the window and saw Fred working. He was building a fence between their two houses. It is eight feet tall.

July 1990

GLORY DENIED

I graduated from Texas Western College in 1958, long before it was the University of Texas at El Paso. We had some good basketball teams in my day, but nothing like the Miners of 1966. I watched that NCAA final game on a black-and-white TV set in Cambridge, Massachussetts, where I was a graduate student at Harvard. I had to explain to my classmates who watched it with me exactly what and where Texas Western College was. None had ever heard of it. But they rooted for Texas Western, and I don't think they did it entirely for my sake. By then, the amazing Miners had captured the interest of the nation. When the 1966 Miners gathered in El Paso to celebrate the 25th anniversary of their accomplishment, Arturo Vasquez, the editor of Nova, the UTEP alumni quarterly, invited me to attend the reunion and write about it for the magazine. A slightly different version of the story was published in the Dallas Morning News, and was reprinted in The Best American Sports Writing: 1992.

As they arrived one by one at the hotel, they shook hands, embraced, kidded each other about gray hair, bald spots, heavier bodies and slower feet. They marveled that a quarter century had passed since the remarkable thing that they had done. They were returning to celebrate the memory of it with their old school and the city. But first they would celebrate with their coach and each other.

"It's great to see all these guys in one place again, to tell the good old war stories," said Nevil Shed. "It makes us feel warm inside to have a city as great as El Paso still remember something that we did for them. And we don't forget what they did for us."

Twenty-five years ago, Coach Don Haskins said, it never entered his mind that they had done anything special. But few who saw it happen would forget it.

For the first time, an all-black team had played an all-white team for the NCAA national basketball championship. The black men had won. History had been made. The Texas Western Miners had changed college basketball forever.

But it was 1966. The march from Selma to Montgomery had happened only a year before, and the struggle for the rights of black people still held the country in turmoil.

Civil rights workers still were being shot. Arsonists still were torching black churches. Gov. George Wallace still was defying a school desegregation order in Alabama. A congressional committee was investigating the Ku Klux Klan. The Georgia Legislature was refusing to seat a newly elected black representative named Julian Bond. Rioting had broken out in a Los Angeles neighborhood called Watts. And Dr. Martin Luther King, Jr. was promising to take the civil rights movement northward to Chicago.

A lot of people in the country didn't like the kind of history that the team from Texas had made.

"I was so young and naive," Coach Haskins remembers. "I hadn't thought of it as putting an all-black team on the court. I was simply playing the best players I had. It's what I had done all year. Then we came home, and the hate mail started pouring in. I got them for months. Thousands of letters, from all over the South."

The letters were only the beginning of his bitter time. A dozen years after winning the greatest athletic triumph in his own life and the history of his school, he would say: "If I could change one thing about my coaching career, I'd wish we came in second in 1966."

* * *

On the night of March 19, 1966, the Texas Western College Miners walked onto a court in College Park, Md., to play the University of Kentucky Wildcats in the final game of the NCAA tournament.

Kentucky had compiled a record of 23 wins and only one loss during the regular season. It was ranked No. 1 in the nation. On the previous evening, in the game that most of the coaches and sportswriters attending the tournament thought would really determine the championship, the Wildcats had beaten the nation's No. 2 team, Duke. If the Wildcats beat the Miners, as almost everybody expected, they would give Kentucky and its legendary 64-year-old coach, Adolph Rupp, their fifth national championship.

The Miners were the "Cinderella team" of the season. Texas Western College — now the University of Texas at El Paso — was a small group of buildings perched on a desert hillside a few hundred yards from the narrow Rio Grande and Mexico. Some 6,000 students were enrolled there. The Miners' 36-year-old coach was in his first college job. A few years earlier, he had been coaching both boys' and girls' basketball at tiny Hedley High School in the Texas Panhandle and doubling as the school bus driver to make ends meet.

Until the 1965-66 season, no one in big-time college basketball had paid much attention to Texas Western. In its entire history it had won only one NCAA tournament game. And at the time it was an "orphan" team, an independent, belonging to no athletic conference. Since none of the major basketball schools had bothered to recruit any of Haskins' players, the Eastern and Midwestern press had dismissed them as "castoffs," "unknowns" and "nondescripts."

But the Miners also had compiled a 23-1 record during the regular season, and when the tournament started, they were ranked No. 3 in the country. After an easy victory over Oklahoma City University in their first tournament game, they had nipped Kansas and Cincinnati, both in overtime, and had beaten Utah in the semifinals to get a crack at Kentucky and the title.

They were upstarts. Traditionally powerful Kentucky and the arrogant Rupp, called "The Baron," were the Establishment. The underdog-lovers of America, watching the tournament on black-and-white TV in living rooms, bars and dormitories, became fascinated with the unknown team from nowhere. But most of the new fans knew absolutely nothing about the school the Miners represented.

"I run into people who remember that game, and they still think I went to an all-black school," said Willie Worsley.

Of course, Texas Western wasn't an all-black college. Far from it. A large percentage of the small group of black students on campus had been recruited from all over the country for their skills at basketball, football, and track. El Paso, where a majority of the citizens are Hispanic and Mexico's fourth-largest city lies over the river, had comparatively few black residents. So did the vast, nearly empty desert region around it.

But 11 years earlier, in 1955, Texas Western had been the first all-white college in Texas — indeed, in the entire old Confederacy — to admit black undergraduates. And in 1956, it had recruited its first black athlete — a basketball player named Charlie Brown.

These steps were taken without fanfare and without incident. And, since El Paso is isolated from the other big Texas cities by miles and miles, and since most of Texas Western's athletic opponents were Southwestern and Western schools that never had been segregated, nobody east of the Pecos noticed, and nobody west of the Pecos cared.

"We were so insulated out here in El Paso that we barely knew all that racial stuff was going on in other places," said David Palacio, one of the players. "We heard about it, I guess, but we didn't think about it."

Nor were the Miners really an all-black team. Of the 12 men on the squad, five — Togo Railey, Jerry Armstrong, David Palacio, Louis Baudoin and Dick Myers — were white. All had played in games during the season, and Armstrong had been instrumental in winning the NCAA semifinal game, coming off the bench to shut down Utah's star shooter, Jerry Chambers.

They and the seven black players were a close-knit group. "We used to drink wine in the dorm together because we didn't have the money to go out," Palacio said. "We used to play a lot of cards. It was friendship, pure friendship. I don't remember a single instance of race being an issue or a problem among us."

But the team's seven best players — Bobby Joe Hill, Orsten Artis, David Lattin, Willie Cager, Harry Flournoy, Nevil Shed and Willie Worsley — were black, and they were the only players who got into the game against the Wildcats, the only Miners seen on TV.

In its entire history, Kentucky had never had a black player. Neither Adolph Rupp nor any other coach in the Southeastern Conference had ever seriously attempted to recruit one.

"It was the first time such a thing had happened," Coach Haskins said, "and it was against mighty Kentucky and The Baron. Had it been against a team with some black players, probably nothing would have been said of it."

Midway through the first quarter, with the Miners leading by one point, Bobby Joe Hill stole the ball, dribbled down the court and made an easy layup. As Kentucky was bringing the ball back up the court, Hill stole it again, dribbled down the court and made another easy layup, giving the Miners a five-point lead. The Wildcats never recovered. Texas Western won, 72-65. For the first time, a Rupp team had been beaten in an NCAA championship game.

"They were a bunch of crooks," he said. "One was on parole from Tennessee State Prison. Two had been kicked out of a junior college in Iowa. Texas Western was suspended by the NCAA for three years after that."

After the game, the Kentucky players — minus their coach — went to the Miners' locker room and congratulated them. "There wasn't any racial thing as far as the two teams were concerned," Artis said.

The next day, 10,000 delirious fans turned out at El Paso International Airport to welcome home the only team from Texas ever to win the NCAA Division I national championship. Willie Cager made a speech: "From all of us to all of you, No. 1 was the best we could do." The crowd went wild. There was a parade through the town.

"It was wonderfully crazy," Willie Worsley said. "The people of El Paso made us feel very special."

"It wasn't until later on," Nevil Shed said, "that we started realizing that this team had opened the doors, not just for blacks but for all minorities, to have an opportunity to play ball at some of the top-notch schools around the United States. What was so beautiful about it was that the very next year things began to open up."

Eventually even Adolph Rupp would recruit a black player. But he was a sore loser. "I hated to see those boys from Texas Western win it," he told the press after the game. "Not because of race or anything like that, but because of the type of recruiting it represents." He hinted that several of Haskins' players had done sinister deeds in the past and that Texas Western had practiced recruiting most foul. A number of sportswriters fell in behind him.

"The title really should belong to Kentucky . . . " wrote an Iowa columnist. "I have heard that one of the top Texas Western players had been charged with a major crime at one time." Since Texas Western was an independent, he wrote, they "can do about as they please in recruiting. They can take rejects from other schools and make them immediately eligible. A school with such low ethics should not be allowed to compete for the national title. Rather it should be in the NBA playoffs."

Rupp's hometown newspaper editorialized that "there is no disgrace in losing to a team such as was assembled by Texas Western after a nationwide search for talent that somehow escaped the recruiters for the Harlem Globetrotters."

As Rupp got older, his loss to Texas Western seemed to gnaw more and more exquisitely, and his descriptions of his villainous opponents grew more and more lurid. In a 1975 interview he said the biggest disappointment of his long career had been losing to "all those ineligible players."

"It wasn't even as close as the score indicates," Orsten Artis said. "At one point we led by 17. Our easiest games in that tournament were the first one, against Oklahoma City, and the last one, against Kentucky."

David Lattin had transferred from Tennessee State University, not the state prison, and Bobby Joe Hill and a player on the Texas Western freshman team — not the championship squad — had transferred from Burlington, Iowa, Junior College. There were no ineligible players on the team. Texas Western had never been suspended by the NCAA for any reason. Indeed, the NCAA had investigated the allegations after the tournament and had given the school a clean bill of health.

"I didn't like us being called misfits, criminals and convicts," Nevil Shed said at the team's reunion. "My mother and father worked hard to bring me up, to make sure that I represented myself in a well-mannered attitude. The people who did that to us didn't really know us. If they had taken the time to look into what 'those seven blacks' were all about, they would have found some pretty impressive guys."

Rupp's vilifications dogged Haskins for years. "I would go to a coaching clinic," he said, "and somebody would come up to me and ask, 'Did you really get that guy out of the pen?'"

But the most serious damage was done in 1968, when *Sports Illustrated* published a five-part series entitled *The Black Athlete*. Part 3, the centerpiece of the series, entitled *In An Alien World*, was devoted entirely to the University of Texas at El Paso (the name of the school had been changed a year earlier) and its alleged exploitation of its black athletes, including the 1966 basketball champions.

"One might suppose that a school which has so thoroughly and actively exploited black athletes would be breaking itself in half to give them something in return, both in appreciation for the achievements of the past and to assure a steady flow of black athletes in the future," wrote its author, Jack Olsen. "One might think that UTEP, with its famed Negro basketball players, its Negro football stars and its predominantly Negro track team would be determined to give its black athletes the very squarest of square deals. But the Negroes on the campus insist this is not the case — far from it."

Olsen went on to describe UTEP and El Paso as a kind of racist hell in which the athletes labored in virtual slavery. The article outraged almost everyone connected with the university. Perhaps El Paso and UTEP hadn't achieved a racial paradise during the turbulent '60s, but, they contended, they had come closer than much of the country and many of its universities.

The athletes said that statements attributed to them in the article had been taken out of context and twisted. A flurry of rebuttal whirled through the local press. UTEP President Joseph Smiley ordered an internal investigation of the school's intercollegiate athletic programs. The investigating committee found no major racial injustices, but recommended a few small reforms, most of them having nothing to do with race.

Olsen and *Sports Illustrated* stood by their article, however, and that made recruiting very hard for Haskins. "Every coach in the country had a copy of that article in his back pocket," he said. "And whenever a black player would indicate an interest in UTEP, they would yank it out and say, 'You don't want to go to El Paso. It's a *horrible* place.'"

In 1975, Neil D. Issacs, a college professor, published a book called *All the Moves: A History of College Basketball*. Relying entirely on Olsen's article as his source, he cited the 1966 Texas Western team as the best example of the abuse of black athletes in America. "There was little in the way of social rewards for them in El Paso," he wrote, "none of them was ever awarded a degree from Texas Western, and they feel that they have lived out the full meaning of exploitation."

A year later, one of America's more famous authors took up the tune, adding a few licks of his own. In *Sports in America*, James A. Michener described the 1966 Miners as "a bunch of loose-jointed ragamuffins" who had been "conscripted" to play basketball in El Paso.

"The El Paso story is one of the most wretched in the history of American sports," he wrote. " . . . I have often thought how much luckier the white players were under Coach Adolph Rupp. He looked after his players; they had a shot at a real education; and they were secure within the traditions of their university, their community and their state. They may have lost the playoff, but they were the winners in every other respect, and their black opponents from El Paso were losers."

Years before Michener's book was published, eight of the 1966 squad — the five whites plus Nevil Shed, Harry Flournoy and Willie Cager — had received their degrees at UTEP. David Lattin had left early because he was drafted by the Phoenix Suns. "He had a year of eligibility left, but I encouraged him to go," Haskins said. "There was a lot of money in it for him, and I kept thinking, 'What if he plays another season for me and ruins a knee or something?'" The remaining three players — Orsten Artis, Bobby Joe Hill and Willie Worsley — had amassed between 78 and 115 semester hours of credit before they dropped out of school to take jobs. Worsley later graduated from the State University of New York.

Michener, who often brags of the amount of research that goes into his massive books, later admitted in a letter to Dr. Mimi Gladstein, a UTEP English professor, that his investigation of the 1966 Miners had gone no farther than the *Sports Illustrated* article. He had consulted neither Haskins nor the players nor even Olsen.

Haskins wanted to sue Michener for libel, but his lawyer talked him out of it. He didn't have the resources, the lawyer said, to fight the author and his publisher, Random House, in the courts.

"I had no fun after winning the national championship," Haskins said.

He's one of the winningest coaches in the game. During his 30 seasons at Texas Western/UTEP his teams have won 579 games and lost 256. Six of his teams have won the Western Athletic Conference championship, five have played in the National Invitational Tournament, and 13 in the NCAA tournament. Crippled by injuries and the scholastic ineligibility of a key player, the Miners didn't make it to the NCAA this year. It was the first time in eight years that they weren't there.

Today Nevil Shed is the director of intramural athletics at the University of Texas at San Antonio; David Lattin is in public relations in Houston; Harry Flournoy is in sales for a baking company in California; Bobby Joe Hill is senior buyer for El Paso Natural Gas in El Paso; Dick Myers is vice president of a clothing manufacturing company in Florida; David Palacio is vice president of Columbia Records in California; Orsten Artis is a detective on the Gary, Ind., police force; the others — Jerry Armstrong, Louis Baudoin, Willie Cager, Togo Railey and Willie Worsley — are teachers and school administrators in Texas, Missouri, New Mexico and New York state.

On the day of the 1991 Miners' last home game and the close of Haskins' 30th season at UTEP, fans by the hundreds would stand in line at El Paso's big shopping malls to have the 1966 champions autograph posters, pictures, pennants and basketballs. Later, during halftime of UTEP's game with New Mexico, the crowd would rise to its feet and cheer the aging heroes once more, and their school would present them with replicas of their old jerseys.

First, though, they would talk deep into the night, reliving their days of glory.

"We won some games while you guys were here," Coach Haskins told them, "but the thing that makes me the happiest is that each and every one of you has turned out to be a fine citizen and a good person and all of you are doing well. That's the most important thing of all."

He's in the twilight of his career, he said. He has mellowed, he said, and is no longer bitter. It's finally sweet to have won.

"It was all a long time ago," he said. "A lot of bridges have been crossed. The entire country has come a long way in the way people think. Tomorrow night, I'm going to start my best five, regardless. And that's what I was doing then."

March 1991

BECAUSE IT'S STILL HERE

For more than 100 years, the people who live in the Davis Mountains have gone about their business - which is ranching - with little interference from the world beyond their horizon. And that's the way they like life to be. Lately, however, the teeming world outside has begun to encroach on them. People in cities far away see the vast open as the perfect place to dump their garbage, sewage and nuclear waste. And the only city in the region, El Paso, is casting a covetous eye upon the only resource the ranchers have - their water. The city of El Paso now owns Ryan Flat and its water. What it will do with it is anybody's guess.

EVEN BEFORE SO MANY PEOPLE LIVED IN THE FAR WESTERN CORNER OF the Trans-Pecos desert, water was scarce. El Paso City Ordinance No. 1, passed at the first meeting of the first City Council in 1873, made it a crime to bathe in the only municipal water supply, an irrigation ditch.

Since then, as El Paso has grown into a city of more than half a million residents and the population of Ciudad Juarez, its sister village across the Rio Grande, has burgeoned to more than a million, the scarcity has constantly worsened.

"El Paso has been mining ground water — taking more out of the ground than rainfall can replace — since 1917," said Ed Archuleta, general manager of El Paso Water Utilities. "In the Hueco Bolson, where we get 65 percent of the water we use, we're now taking water out 20 times faster than nature can recharge it."

The Census Bureau estimates that El Paso will be a city of 1.1 million by the year 2040. How large Juarez, which gets its water from the same underground source, will be by that time is beyond anyone's guess.

And since the water scarcity is growing even faster than the metropolitan area, it has begun to inspire fear and worry in people far beyond the city limits, among the ranches and small towns that share the vast, arid Trans-Pecos with Texas' fourth-largest city. El Paso is casting a covetous eye in their direction.

In the city, which gets only seven or eight inches of rainfall in a normal year, the problem has become inescapable. Billboards urge residents to conserve, and water makes Page One of the morning paper every day: "Water odd," the headline reads on Wednesday, Friday and Sunday. "Houses with addresses ending in odd numbers may water today, except from 9 a.m. to 7 p.m." Every Tuesday, Thursday and Saturday, the headline reads: "Water even."

Environmental enforcement officers patrol the streets looking for violators. And, under a new water conservation ordinance, residents who are caught watering their yards on the wrong day — or hosing down the driveway, or washing the car without a bucket or a shut-off nozzle on the hose — may be fined $50 to $500. The rules are permanent and are enforced year-round.

Despite the conservation efforts, it's estimated that the Hueco Bolson will be sucked dry in 35 years, and El Paso is forced to look elsewhere for new sources of supply. The city's Water Resource Management Plan, in which problems and possible solutions over the next

50 years are projected, calls for greatly increased use of water from the Rio Grande and more recycling of waste water, which would be purified to drinking-water standards and then pumped back into the ground to recharge the Hueco Bolson.

But it's the city's search for new water outside El Paso County that's causing anger and unease in the sparsely populated counties of the Trans-Pecos.

"The fear is, El Paso is water-starved and it's getting desperate," said Jeff Davis County Bob Dillard in Fort Davis. "The fear is, they're coming to get our water, and the lives of the people here will mean nothing to them. The fear is that they'll drink the cup, and when it's empty they'll go find some more somewhere else."

El Paso spent $8 million and 10 years suing the state of New Mexico for the right to drill for water in the nearby Mesilla Bolson and pipe it across the state line. When the suit failed, the city turned its efforts toward its weaker — and almost equally dry — neighbors in Texas.

Last month, the city's Public Service Board, parent body of El Paso Water Utilities, announced a contingency contract for the $2 million purchase of a 25,000-acre farm 150 miles from the city in Jeff Davis and Presidio counties.

Under the land in the Ryan Aquifer, the board believes, is enough water to supply 80 million gallons a day to El Paso for 17 years.

Under its contract with the seller, Connecticut General Life Insurance Co., the Public Service Board will drill several test wells on Antelope Valley Farms, as the tract is called, to determine whether its estimates of the quality and quantity of the water are accurate. If they are, the sale will be completed.

"What scares people here is that El Paso has put that year amount on it," Judge Dillard said. "They say it's a 17-year supply. The question is: What happens after the 17 years? Once the water is gone, what do we have left?"

The Ryan Aquifer is believed to be a basin of ice age water trapped deep below the surface of the earth. It extends under a sizable portion of western Jeff Davis and northern Presidio counties and is the only source of water for the small town of Valentine, near the Jeff Davis-Presidio county line, and a number of ranches in the mountains and flats. Its recharge rate, from an average rainfall of about 14 inches a year, is very low, estimated by the U.S. Geological Survey to be about 5,800 acre-feet annually.

If El Paso were to pump the projected 80 million gallons a day, the annual recharge would provide the city only a 23-day supply of water. After that, the pumps would be mining water, and the water table would begin dropping.

Antelope Valley Farms has been a worry to area residents ever since the late 1970s, when Olsen Farms, a subsidiary of Connecticut

General, bought the acreage and converted it from grazing land to irrigated crop land.

Albert Miller, a neighboring rancher who also operates the municipal water system for Valentine, a town of about 200, believes the operation has affected the water table significantly during periods of heavy irrigation, especially in years of little rainfall.

"In 1989, we had only 6½ inches of rain at the ranch," he said. "And Antelope Valley was pumping real hard. The pump on Valentine's city well started pumping air. I had to lower it almost 100 feet to get water."

Indeed, it was the high cost of pulling water from hundreds of feet within the earth with diesel-powered pumps, Mr. Miller said, that made Antelope Valley's crops of beans, corn, wheat and milo unprofitable. Eventually the operation went bankrupt, and Connecticut General has been trying to rid itself of the property for years.

"Some people in the area think El Paso buying the land is better than the alternative," Judge Dillard said. "It was rumored that the city of Houston or the state of New Jersey was interested in buying the land and using it as a place to dispose of their sewer sludge. But a lot of the ranchers, especially the younger ones, are just as alarmed at what El Paso might do."

"I'm really apprehensive," said Chile Ridley, whose family has ranched across the highway from the Antelope Valley site for generations. "Are all of us out here going to have to deepen our wells in order to run livestock on our land and get drinking water? What about all the wildlife that's dependent on our windmills and stock tanks?

"Is El Paso going to suck the water away from Valentine? Will it affect Marfa? What will it do to the springs in the Davis Mountains? What will it do to the springs below the rimrock, down near the river? Nobody has done a study of the effects that much pumping is likely to have on the land or on us. We're all extremely concerned. Without water, our land's not worth a flip."

Although Trans-Pecos ranchers tend to be highly independent folk who loathe government regulation and bureaucracy, Mr. Miller, Mr. Ridley, and others have asked the officials of their counties to investigate the possibility of forming an underground water conservation district in hopes that it could regulate and limit the amount of water El Paso could remove from the ground.

"You've got a willing seller and a willing buyer here," Mr. Ridley said. "You've got private property rights. You've got to respect that. But you're talking about a resource that we have conserved over the years and treated with respect, which they haven't done in El Paso. And the reason they want it is because it's still here. So we're in a battle."

Jeff Davis County Attorney Ann Barker said dozens of residents of all parts of the Davis Mountains area have phoned her and even come to her door to express their worry. But their legal options appear bleak so far.

"An underground water conservation district may not afford us much protection from what El Paso is contemplating," she said. "Such districts mainly control the flow of water within an area by permitting procedures and well-spacing requirements, but they don't really restrict anyone from removing water from property they own.

"And we just don't have the budget to go get a crackerjack water lawyer from Austin or Dallas or Houston to fight this for us. This is a county with a total annual budget of around $500,000. So who's going to look out for these citizens?"

Bill Colbert, public information officer for the Texas Water Commission, confirmed that Ms. Barker's fears are well-grounded.

"The way the current state law is structured, ground water belongs to the property owner," he said. "It's like a mineral right. The landowner can take as much as he wants out of the ground, even if his neighbor's wells are drying up."

Mr. Archuleta of El Paso Water Utilities calls Texas water law "the law of the biggest pump." And in the Ryan Aquifer, El Paso's pump would be the biggest by far. But he says the residents of the rural counties are worrying prematurely.

"Because that's a finite source of water out there, it's not in our 50-year plan," he said. "If we can buy more tracts of land in the same area, it might be economical, in time, to build the pipeline and pumping stations necessary to bring that water to El Paso. But our plan now is to purchase it and then just kind of hold it for many, many years, probably."

The people of Jeff Davis and Presidio counties don't believe El Paso's reassurances. "We hear the horror stories from up there, about people not having water and sewers in southern El Paso County," said Judge Dillard. "If they buy this land, I don't see how they can wait long to come get the water."

And Jeff Davis County's worry already is spreading to neighboring Culberson County, where El Paso is rumored to be eying land in Lobo Flat, between Valentine and Van Horn.

At a recent meeting of the Rio Grande Council of Governments, Culberson County Judge John Conoly buttonholed an El Paso County commissioner and told him, "If you try to come and take our water, we'll be waiting for you at the county line."

"We're not just going to sit here and let them come and take it away from us," Judge Conoly said later. "We'll fight them with whatever resources we can muster."

September 1991

THE REAL PEPPER-UPPER

It's strange, the things that stick in your memory from your early childhood, and the things that slip away without a trace. I'm sure more important things than an occasional trip to the Dr Pepper plant in Dublin, Texas, must have happened to me when I was a small boy, but few events remain more vivid in my mind. When I returned, almost 50 years later, I was amazed and reassured to discover how accurate my memory had been.

I WOULD HAVE STOOD AT THE WINDOW ALL DAY IF MOTHER HAD LET me, watching the bottles move by. To me they looked like soldiers, marching single file. World War II was raging then, and soldiers were much on the minds of everyone, even children. Almost anything could remind us of soldiers.

Now, nearly 50 years later, through the same plate glass window, the bottles still look like soldiers to me, marching along, their heads bobbing. But it's no longer the resemblance that enthralls me, it's the fact that I've come to look at something that I haven't seen in half a century, and it's still as I remembered it.

I remember the heat as vividly as the bottles. Cotton basking in the fields, locusts whirring in the trees, the hot wind blasting through the open windows of the car, we children cranky and fighting and crying on the back seat, sweat rolling down our naked chests, our mother pleading, threatening: "If you don't straighten up and behave, I won't buy you a cold drink."

Those trips from our farm near Carlton, Texas, to Dublin, some 20 miles away, must have been hell for her. And they must have been necessary in the extreme, for gas was rationed and new tires were impossible to come by. We didn't travel for frivolous reasons.

While Mother did her business in the stores and offices of Dublin, we kids had to wait in the car. The car that had been hot when it was moving became an oven parked on the shadeless street. We suffered. To make our suffering bearable, we teased each other, fought each other, threatened to tell on each other.

But we wouldn't have missed a trip to Dublin for the world, for at the end, just as we were starting back to the farm, Mother would pull the car up to the Dr Pepper bottling plant at Elm and Patrick streets. We would get out and stand at the window and watch the bottles march along the company's little bottling line while Mother went inside and bought us each a Dr Pepper out of the wooden, metal-lined box of melting ice that stood near the doorway.

Then we would climb back into the car and begin the journey home.

The hot wind still blasted us, sweat still rolled down our bellies, but we no longer were miserable. Our lives had been transformed by the wet bottles in our hands and the icy liquid that coursed down our parched throats like a torrent of joy.

In today's air-conditioned summers, there is no ecstasy so intense as that tiny splash of cold into our relentlessly torrid world. None at all.

This time I have driven the 100 miles from Dallas without sweating, even though the heat, when I emerge from my air-conditioned car, is as heavy and aggressive as I remembered. And this time I get to do what I never got to do when I was a child. I get to go inside the building where the bottles are marching.

Bill Kloster, who has worked at the plant for 58 years and now has inherited it from its previous owner, Grace Lyons, who died on the 100th anniversary of its opening, is in his small office, tending to his mail and phone orders. He gets two or three a day, he says, from all over the country, most of them from displaced Texans. Today's orders are from New York, California, Illinois and Nevada.

"It costs $15.27 for a case, including the deposit for the bottles and the wooden case," he says. "The UPS charges can run up to 25 or 30 dollars. But they're willing to pay it. They've got to have it."

What the lonesome expatriates have got to have is Dr Pepper. But not the kind of Dr Pepper that you and I buy in aluminum cans at the supermarket.

They crave the kind of Dr Pepper that Mother placed into my hand at this same spot nearly 50 years ago. The kind that's made nowhere in the world anymore but in Mr. Kloster's plant. Dr Pepper brewed with pure cane sugar instead of corn syrup or NutraSweet and put up in thick glass 6½-ounce and 10-ounce bottles that must be opened with a bottle opener and are returned to the plant empty to be refilled again and again.

Mr. Kloster takes me into the sacred room, where three men are working the magic machine. One of them is taking dirty bottles from their wooden cases, inspecting them for chips and cracks and feeding them into a slot in the machine.

"The bottles go the length of this machine in hot alkali water," Mr. Kloster says. "The alkali is strong. If you dropped some of it on your leather boot there, it would burn a hole in it. People put kerosene, brake fluid and everything else in these bottles. It has to be strong to sterilize them. Then the bottles come over here and get rinsed, then they come out clean over there."

As they leave the washer, the bottles line up in single file and begin their march, first to one of the three syrupers for a squirt of the Dr Pepper syrup concocted by Mr. Kloster himself from a secret formula, then to one of the 20 filling heads for a larger squirt of carbonated water, then on to one of the three crowners, where their little caps are clamped on.

Then the bottles bob merrily into a machine that whisks them about in a little dance that mixes the syrup and the water, then on to the inspection station, where a man checks them for correct color and places them into their ancient wooden cases by hand.

There are 459 other Dr Pepper bottling plants across the country and other parts of the world now, but they're Johnnys-come-lately compared to this one, the oldest of them all.

Wade Morrison and Charles Alderton invented the divine elixir at the Old Corner Drug Store in Waco and named it for Dr. Charles T. Pepper of Rural Retreat, Virginia, the father of Mr. Morrison's beloved, in vain hope that the honor would help Mr. Morrison win the lady's hand. Just six years later, in 1891, Sam Houston Prim, a Dublin dealer in feed, coal, and ice, was given distribution rights to Dr Pepper within a forty-mile radius of the town.

Mr. Kloster does business out of the same building that Mr. Prim did, and still services the same area. "We go as far as Tolar, Hico, Hamilton, Iredell, Comanche, De Leon, Gorman and Desdemona," he says.

He went to work at the plant in 1933, when he was 14 years old, sorting bottles for a dime an hour. "My father died when I was 11," he says. "I had two brothers and three sisters, and my mother was left without any money except what she could get taking in washing and things like that. Being the oldest, I had to help out. I mowed lawns and worked at the variety store, then I came over here."

When Mr. Prim died in 1946, his daughter, Mrs. Lyons, took over the company and made Mr. Kloster the manager. Since then, Dr Pepper has been not only his business, but his passion. When the parent company abandoned returnable bottles and began using throw-away aluminum cans and plastic bottles, he kept filling the returnable bottles. When the parent company gave up cane sugar for cheaper corn syrup, he continued using sugar. He feels strongly about it:

"My wife used to fuss at me. 'You're wasting money,' she would say. But Mr. Prim always said we should never change the way we blended our sweetener with the Dr Pepper concentrate. And we haven't."

Three rooms of the plant are full of Dr Pepper memorabilia that Mr. Kloster has collected over the years — signs, clocks, calendars, trays, mirrors, lamps, posters, thermometers, bottles that have held Dr Pepper at various periods of its history, a soda fountain from an old Dublin drugstore and photographs of Mr. Prim and Mrs. Lyons.

On his own signs and bottle caps, Mr. Kloster still uses some of the old advertising slogans that the parent company abandoned many years ago: "Drink a Bite to Eat at 10, 2 and 4," with the three-handed clock pointing to the hours when we're most likely to need a friendly pepper-upper. "Three Times to Enjoy Life More: 10, 2 and 4." "Good for Life." "King of Beverages." "Just What the Doctor Ordered," with its picture of the doctor wearing a top hat and monocle.

And, of course, there's the ineffable bottling machine, a clattering marvel containing nothing the least bit computerish or electronic in its whole blessed body. "The bottle soaker was bought new in '47," Mr. Kloster says. "We've been using the bottling machine since the '30s. It's the only one of its kind still operating in the United States. We can't get parts for it, so we have to do a lot of welding and improvising."

And, in a country that's suffocating in throw-away packaging, the reusable 6½-ounce and 10-ounce bottles that the machine fills are no longer manufactured. So when the 500-and-some-odd cases now in use are broken, thrown away or disappear into antique collections, that will be the end of really real Dr Pepper.

Meanwhile, on the desk beside me stands a bottle made of thick light green glass. I pick it up. It fits my hand just right, and has a pleasant heft to it. I sip. The flavor is dark and rich. If this were wine, it would come from France and cost a lot of money.

Even in this air-conditioned office, without a cotton field in sight and not a whisper of a locust, it's a torrent of joy.

September 1991

MEMORIES OF SELMA

Most of us could tell a story or two about events in our past that we consider landmarks in our lives, pivotal happenings that took us off the course we were on and set us on another. Usually, we don't recognize those events for what they are until years later, when we can look back and see the points at which the directions of our lives were changed. But sometimes, something happens to you, and you know at once that you will never be the same. You catch yourself in the act of becoming a different person. For me, the march from Selma to Montgomery in 1965 was such an event. That march also was the most historically significant event that I have ever witnessed as a participant, and not as a professional observer. I'm glad I was there. This memoir was published on the 25th anniversary of the final day of the march. It's based on a journal I kept.

SOMETIMES THE SHERIFF STANDING ON THE COURTHOUSE STEPS WOULD tell them the registrar was sick and hadn't come to work. Sometimes he would say they had arrived too late, that the registrar had already locked his office and gone home. Sometimes he would say they had come on the wrong day. Sometimes he didn't bother with an explanation. He just told them to leave.

But sometimes a black person would be allowed into the registration office to fill out the application form and take the test that the State of Alabama required of citizens who wanted to vote.

The test was pretty much what the registrar wanted to make it. White applicants might be asked to read their names, or the first word of the U.S. Constitution: "We." Black applicants might be asked: "What part does the Vice President play in the Senate and the House?" or "What legal and legislative steps would the State of Alabama and the State of Mississippi have to take to combine into one state?" The registrar decided who passed the test and who didn't.

In Dallas County, Ala., in 1965, more than half the citizens were black, but only about 300 of them had been allowed to register to vote. The marches to the courthouse in Selma had added almost none to their number.

In neighboring Lowndes and Wilcox counties, where black people outnumbered white people four to one, not a single black person had registered to vote in 65 years.

The small drama at the courthouse steps had been playing almost daily since early January, when the Rev. Frederick D. Reese, the Selma pastor who had organized the Dallas County Voters League, asked Dr. Martin Luther King Jr. and the Southern Christian Leadership Conference to lead a registration drive.

Dr. King's intermittent presence in Selma put the courthouse marches on the network news, but the would-be voters always were turned away at the steps, or were told to wait in line all day and then were sent home.

After church on Sunday, March 7, about 500 marchers led by the Rev. Hosea Williams of the SCLC moved through the streets, singing *We Shall Overcome* and shouting: "Free-dom! Free-dom!" They said they were going to march all the way to Montgomery, 54 miles away, and lay their grievances before Gov. George Wallace. They weren't prepared for such a march. Some of the women were wearing high-heeled shoes. But they had started.

At the Edmund Pettus Bridge, which carries U.S. 80 across the Alabama River on the edge of downtown Selma, helmeted state troopers and sheriff's deputies were standing on the sidewalk and in the highway, blocking the way to Montgomery. Some carried clubs, some tear gas guns, some electric cattle prods. Some — members of Sheriff Jim Clark's special volunteer "posse" — rode horses. Some of them carried bullwhips.

Col. Al Lingo, the commander of the state troopers, ordered the marchers to disperse. When they didn't, the troopers and deputies fell upon them. They swung their clubs. They fired tear gas into the crowd. They trampled women and children under their horses. They lashed at the fallen bodies with their bullwhips. The horsemen pursued the fleeing marchers back into the town, all the way to the church where they had begun. When the melee ended, 60 black people had been injured.

Americans had never seen anything quite like that on the evening news. By Sunday night, several hundred volunteers, among them ministers, priests and students from all parts of the country, were on their way to Selma to join the struggle. One of them was the Rev. James Reeb, a young Unitarian pastor from Boston.

On Tuesday evening, Mr. Reeb and another minister ate dinner in a restaurant in downtown Selma. They finished their meal and walked out onto the sidewalk. A gang of men ran out of the darkness and beat them with clubs.

Two days later, James Reeb died.

His death was one of the reasons I went. I can't say he was my friend, exactly, but I knew him. He had taken a course or two at Harvard Divinity School, where I was a graduate student. After class he would go to the refectory and drink coffee and shoot the breeze, as we all did. The divinity school is the smallest school at Harvard. We all knew almost everybody there.

The horses and the whips had something to do with it, too. In the early 1960s, we had become almost accustomed to seeing police attack civil rights demonstrators with clubs and tear gas on our newscasts, but the horses and bullwhips were new. What kind of police officer would trample a child under a horse's hooves? What kind of police used bullwhips?

And I went because I believed that Dr. King and the demonstrations were in the right. A few years earlier, when I was a student at Brite Divinity School at Texas Christian University, I was one of a committee that met with the university chancellor and urged him to allow TCU's few black students to live in the dorms and eat in the university dining hall if they wished. And I had walked a picket line in front of a movie theater in downtown Fort Worth, demanding that the management allow black patrons to sit wherever they wished, not just in the balcony.

I wasn't one of the shock troops of the civil rights movement, but I believed.

And I went because I was tired of being ill at ease that I was a white Southerner, a descendant of Confederate soldiers, living among self-righteous Yankees who believed that the nation's only race problem was in the South, and who suspected that anyone who talked with a drawl was a Klansman in his heart. I wanted to prove to them that many white Southerners believed in freedom and equality and justice, too.

And I went because I loved the South and wanted to see its tragic racial conflicts resolved without further bloodshed. I didn't want any more people to have to die so that all adult Americans could vote.

So on the night of March 15, when two chartered buses loaded with students from Boston's four Protestant theological schools headed south, I was aboard. Our arrangement with the bus company called for us to ride to Selma, show our support, stay until the afternoon of March 19, then return to Boston. We hoped the big push to the capital would begin while we were there, but the matter was in the hands of U.S. District Judge Frank Johnson in Montgomery, and he hadn't decided yet whether to allow such a march.

We arrived in Selma about 7 a.m. on March 17, groggy from 34 hours on the road. Volunteers led us off in small groups to homes and churches open to us as living quarters. A young boy took me and two other Harvard students — Roy Branson and Bob Schraeder — to the Green Street Baptist Church. We unrolled our sleeping bags on the floor of a Sunday school room and tried to sleep. We couldn't.

That afternoon we joined 500 demonstrators who were moving in double file toward the courthouse. The sky had turned dark and threatening. My marching partner was a black girl who said her name was Easter, about 12 years old. She was shy, or maybe just quiet. I asked her how many of the marches she had been in. She said, "All of them we've had." I asked her if she had been at the Pettus Bridge. She said, "Yes." She had two small scars on her face. I wondered if she had received them in the marches, but I wasn't bold enough to ask.

Just as we arrived at the courthouse, the dark skies opened. Heavy rain and hail pelted us. Easter had a colorful plaid umbrella. She opened it, and I held it over us. Not many of the marchers had had her foresight. A young black man standing next to us was getting soaked. We invited him under the umbrella, too.

Several black ministers stood on the courthouse steps and said prayers. The Rev. Hosea Williams, who had led the marchers to the Pettus Bridge on what was now being called "Bloody Sunday," made a speech. I remember nothing of what he said, just the rain and the hail and the smirks on the faces looking at us through the courthouse windows, happy at our soaking. We stayed a long time, I think. Then we sang several freedom songs and began our walk back to Brown Chapel AME Church, where all the marches started.

State troopers were swarming over the downtown area. I counted seven of their cars on a single block. Two troopers were in each. White men stood in groups under the awnings in front of the stores, shouting as we walked by: "Nigger lover!" "White nigger!" Easter and I, walking together under the plaid umbrella, seemed especially to anger them. A man said: "Look at that preacher and his nigger gal! Ain't they cute?"

Twenty-five years later, I remember his face. He was the first to show me hatred in person.

Judge Johnson decided that day to allow the march to Montgomery. He ordered the Alabama State Troopers not only to refrain from attacking the marchers, but to protect them. If they failed, he warned, they would be held in contempt of court.

The judge placed restrictions on the marchers, too. About 40 of the 54 miles of highway between Selma and the capitol in Montgomery were only two lanes wide. Along that stretch, the judge said, no more than 300 people could march, and one lane of the highway must always be kept open to traffic.

So the plan became this: The march would begin at Brown Chapel on March 21 after an outdoor church service. The crowd of black Selma citizens and the volunteers then would march out of the city as far as the four-lane pavement extended, about eight miles. Then all but 300 marchers would return to Selma.

The 300 would march for three days until the highway widened to four lanes again, a few miles outside Montgomery. Then the throng would rejoin them for the push to the capitol, where, it was hoped, Dr. King and Mr. Reese and the other leaders would meet with Gov. Wallace.

About 250 of the 300 would be local people who had fought the voting rights battle in Selma for many months, even years. The remaining 50 would be celebrities who had raised money to support the march, dignitaries who had lent their names and reputations to the cause, and a few volunteers from around the country whose work for civil rights had been long and hard.

When our buses headed back to Boston on March 19, Roy and Bob and I weren't aboard. We couldn't bear to leave Selma just as the greatest march of the civil rights struggle was about to begin. We weren't among the honored 300, but there was plenty of work to do. Soon after Judge Johnson handed down his order, the black section of Selma came to resemble the staging area for an invasion. Dozens of trucks moved in and out, delivering food, air mattresses, tents, medical supplies, portable toilets. Many of the cargoes came from other states, since Alabama suppliers refused to sell or rent to the cause.

Lines of chartered buses stopped in front of the churches, bringing hundreds of new volunteers for the big march. Most were white, most of them clergy and professors and students, some from as far away as Hawaii. Cheers greeted them all. Reporters, photographers and TV crews were arriving from all over the world. It was raining every day.

In the churchyards, Hosea Williams and other veterans were teaching us how to fall to the ground, roll up in a ball and cup our hands over our genitals. "They always try to hit you there first," Mr. Williams said. "If they can't hit you there, they'll go for the head and the kidneys, but you can't protect everything."

He told us to carry identification and at least $2 at all times, so we wouldn't be arrested for vagrancy. He told us to carry no aspirin or prescription medicines, so we wouldn't be arrested for possession of drugs, and no pocketknives, nail files or ballpoint pens, so we wouldn't be jailed for carrying deadly weapons.

State troopers, Dallas County deputies and Selma policemen sat in their cars near the street corners, watching us.

Those of us not among the 300 were assigned jobs preparing food, driving trucks, finding phones for the reporters to use, carrying messages, raising tents. Roy and Bob and I were among those assigned to be marshals.

The marshals were to wear yellow armbands and walk outside the ranks and keep order among the marchers on the big day. We were to keep our people away from the roadsides, so hostile onlookers couldn't grab them, pull them away and beat them or kill them. We were to help stragglers and find ways to get them safely out of the march and back home. We were to keep our people from answering the jeers and curses they would hear. We were to keep them looking straight ahead.

Sunday was sunny and warm. Three thousand of us stood in the street in front of Brown Chapel, in the midst of the George Washington Carver Homes public housing project. On the church steps was a lectern covered with a white cloth. Smoke from a garbage fire drifted around the side of the church. Cinders were falling on the crowd. Dr. King was speaking.

"You will be the people that will light a new chapter in the history books of our nation," he said. "This is one of the greatest demonstrations for human rights in history. We have waited for freedom. We are tired of waiting. Now is the time. Walk together, children. Don't you get weary. And it will lead us to the Promised Land. And Alabama will be a new Alabama, and America will be a new America."

Then, marching eight abreast, we started.

Downtown, a segregated crowd lined the sidewalks, white people on one side of the street, black people on the other. They were shouting. "White nigger!" "Communist!" "Scum!" "Yes!" "Freedom!" "Praise God!"

I was walking on the white side of the street, down the narrow space between the marchers and the crowd. A man stepped off the sidewalk and grabbed my arm. He tried to rip off my marshal's armband. "What the hell does all this damn stuff mean?" he said. I looked him in the eyes and said nothing, as I had been trained to do. I slowly pulled my arm from his grasp. He stepped back onto the sidewalk, and I walked on.

A police car was at the corner where we turned onto Broad Street, Selma's main thoroughfare. A recording of *Dixie* blared from the car's loudspeaker. Then *Bye Bye Blackbird*. A policeman standing beside the car made a big show of taking pictures — or pretending to — of local black people in the march. "We know who you are. We'll remember you," he said.

When we crossed Edmund Pettus Bridge, I noticed the federal presence for the first time. National guardsmen and regular Army MPs were everywhere. Military helicopters circled over us.

Gov. Wallace had claimed that Alabama lacked the resources to protect the marchers as Judge Johnson had ordered, so President Lyndon Johnson had nationalized the Alabama guard and sent the MPs from Fort Benning, Ga. Soldiers stood in pairs — a black and a white in each pair — all along the highway, bayonets fixed to their rifles.

Beyond the bridge, crowds of white people leaned into the road, shouting so loudly that we could hear nothing else. The nuns among us bore the worst. What the white women by the roadside screamed about their chastity can't be repeated here. Some of the men by the roadside were drunk. For a quarter of a mile, I almost held my breath, afraid they would pull me or someone from our column into their midst.

Then suddenly we were in the countryside, passing pastures and fields and woods and small communities where whites and blacks stood together by the road, the whites shouting insults, the blacks singing.

Cars crowded the other half of the four-lane highway. Many bore signs: "Coonsville, U.S.A." "Go Home, Scum." Teenagers leaning from car windows waved Confederate flags. Where a country lane opened into the highway, two guardsmen stood, one white, one black. The white soldier glared with rage. Tears rolled down the black soldier's face.

We reached the camping ground — a plot of land owned by a black farmer, eight miles from Selma — just before sundown. The temperature was dropping fast and thunderclouds were gathering. The leaders canceled the mass rally that had been scheduled, and the marchers, except for the 300, were shuttled by bus to a special train, which would return them to Selma.

A young black man invited Bob and me to ride back to town in his car with him and two of his friends. It would be faster than the train, so we accepted. We got into the back seat with one of the friends.

As we crossed the Edmund Pettus Bridge, the driver told Bob and me to crouch down so we couldn't be seen through the windows. Just as we reached the heart of downtown, the engine died. The driver coasted the car around a corner off Broad Street and parked it.

"It's the generator," he said. "It's been giving trouble. I'll go call somebody to come get us." He told Bob and me to hunker on the floor of the back seat, then he went away.

A few minutes later, he returned. He said he had found a phone, but it was out of order. He tried to start the car again. It wouldn't. He left to look for another phone.

Everybody was tense. "If the troopers see you in this car with us, they'll kill us all," said the man in the front seat. Then a car door slammed. "Oh, God, It's deputies!" he whispered.

A flashlight glared at the window. What you boys doing?" It was more a threat than a question.

"Car busted," mumbled the man in the front seat. "My friend has gone to look for another one."

"What's wrong with it?" the deputy asked.

"Don't know. It just stopped."

The deputy flashed his light into the face of the man in the back seat with Bob and me. At that moment, I *knew* with absolute certainty that we were going to be killed. But my mind was full of a calm that I hadn't known before — a tranquility I still can't explain. It was as if I were standing outside myself, watching myself as I would a character in a movie, not at all grieved that he was about to die.

Then the light moved away. "Well, all right," the deputy said. The door slammed again. The police car pulled away. The man in the front seat said, "There was two of them. Lord."

In a while, our driver returned with another car. His friends hustled Bob and me into the back seat. We stuck to the back streets and eased back to Brown Chapel.

The next two days moved slowly for Roy and Bob and me. We read, slept and stayed up almost all of Tuesday night playing poker. Roy, a Seventh Day Adventist, had to be taught the game. It was raining again. I was fighting a cold, probably the result of that first rainy walk to the courthouse with Easter.

Things being as they were, I couldn't go to any of the drugstores in Selma, all owned by whites. A small boy told me about an old man who had a tiny store in a tin shed and took me there. The man had one box of Anacin and one bottle of Vicks cough syrup. I bought them, doctored myself, and contrary to Hosea Williams' orders, kept them with me in my coat pocket.

In the mornings, after the 300 were on the road again, we would ride out on trucks and help clean up their campsite. The days were wet and cold. The mud was deep and black and sticky. I had a fever.

About 4 p.m. on Wednesday, March 24, Roy and Bob and I climbed aboard an enclosed truck with about 50 black people and a couple of other whites to ride to the last night's encampment at the City of St.

Jude, a Catholic hospital-school complex just inside the Montgomery city limits. When we arrived, a large crowd already was milling about the tents and trucks, waiting for the big show that singer Harry Belafonte had put together to entertain the marchers. The people were searching for dry spots to sit and eat the sack lunches that were being distributed, but rain earlier in the day had made the place a quagmire.

Everything was going wrong. The lights and sound equipment which Mr. Belafonte had sent from New York to Montgomery had wound up in New Orleans. At 7:30, when darkness had fallen and the show was supposed to begin, a work crew still was trying to rig makeshift lights and speakers on the stage, which was built of coffin boxes.

As the crowd grew, it became restless. The people in back began to push the people in front closer and closer toward the stage. The marshals surrounded the stage and locked arms to try to keep the crowd back, but we couldn't. Soon we were crushed against the coffin boxes. Then, when we managed to move the people who were crushing us back a few feet, they were crushed between us and those who were pushing from behind. After two hours of this, when it seemed that our arms were about to be pulled from their sockets, the lights came on, Mr. Belafonte stepped onto the stage, the crowd calmed, and the show began at last.

Sammy Davis, Jr., Shelley Winters, Dick Gregory, Leonard Bernstein, Billy Eckstine, Alan King, Anthony Perkins, Tony Bennett, Odetta, Nina Simone, James Baldwin, Peter, Paul and Mary, the Chad Mitchell Trio and about 20 more celebrities performed or made short speeches. So did Dr. Ralph Bunche, Dr. King and other leaders of the movement.

When the show ended, I went to pick up my gear for the ride to the First CME Church, where the marshals had been assigned to eat and sleep. My overcoat was missing. It was old and not much of a loss, but my Anacin and cough medicine were in its pockets.

By the time my friends and I got to the church, all the food was gone, and every square foot of the basement, sanctuary, pews, balcony, chancel and classrooms were covered with sleeping bodies. We finally found a tiny storeroom on the third floor that had only one occupant. We unrolled our sleeping bags and lay down without bothering to take off our clothes or even get inside the bags.

It was 3:30 a.m.

I looked forward and couldn't see the beginning of the column. I looked back and couldn't see the end. Marchers were streaming into the column from the side streets like tributaries flowing into a great river. Many wore their church clothes. Well-wishers lined the streets. Kindergarten children on the sidewalks were singing freedom songs, led by their teachers. Ancient, toothless women grinned and waved at us from their porches.

The mood of the marchers was different from what it had been when the march started Sunday. Then, our mood was quiet determination. We had walked in silence, ignoring the jeers and taunts of those who hated us. But now our determination had become triumph, and the streets echoed with shouts, freedom songs, hymns and laughter. "Come on!" the marchers shouted to the onlookers. "Come on! We're not afraid!"

There were 25,000 of us now. As we neared downtown, only a few white people watched us from the sidewalks, but the windows of stores and offices were full of faces. There were fewer insults, or maybe they were just harder to hear over our own tumult. A meek-looking little man with a frightened grin on his face stood in the street and held a small Confederate flag above his head.

Some were on our side. A white boy ran out of a restaurant carrying two soft drinks and gave them to two black women just ahead of me. "Pass these around to your friends," he said. Then he went and stood on the sidewalk, smiling. He was about 18 years old.

At last we reached the plaza of Dexter Avenue. There stood the beautiful white capitol, gleaming in the sun. The Alabama and Confederate flags flew at the top of its dome. The Stars and Stripes were nowhere visible. On the porch stood many official-looking men. Gov. Wallace wasn't among them. He was in his office, we learned later, watching from behind the slats of the Venetian blinds.

On the capitol porch lay a large slab of plywood. Several green-helmeted state troopers were standing on it. The wood covered a brass plaque marking the spot where Jefferson Davis took his oath of office as president of the Confederacy 104 years earlier. I heard later that the troopers were afraid Dr. King might stand on it and make his speech from there. But he and the other leaders were on a flatbed truck near the foot of the capitol steps. The Rev. Ralph Abernathy stepped to the microphone and said: "I'd like to sing the national anthem, but I don't see an American flag here." Instantly, hundreds of flags, large and small, rose above the crowd.

"We have been drenched by the rain," Dr. King said. "Our bodies are tired. Our feet are sore. They told us we wouldn't get here. And there are those who said we would get here over their dead bodies."

"Speak!" the crowd said. "Speak!"

"Segregation is on its death bed in Alabama," he said, "and the only thing uncertain about it is how costly the segregationists and Wallace will make the funeral."

When he finished, we sang *We Shall Overcome*, and suddenly it was over. The crowd began breaking up. The troops who had protected us were released from duty. Bob and Roy and I, carrying our gear, followed the stream of people a few blocks, then began asking the way to the Greyhound station.

We turned a corner and suddenly we were alone in white Montgomery. Three white men were following us, shouting. They followed us for blocks. Then three young black men standing at a street corner saw us and heard them and understood what was happening. "Would you like us to walk with you where you're going?" one of them asked.

"Yes, we would," I said.

Soon the white men faded away and we were safely inside the station. Two hours later, our bus departed. Nearly all the passengers had been in the march. One of them had a radio. Not long after we left Montgomery, he said, "Oh, God. There's been a murder."

It was Viola Liuzzo, 39 years old, mother of five, from Detroit. She lived in the Green Street Baptist Church, where we lived. She had been one of the hardest workers among us. While she was driving from Selma to Montgomery, still working after the march, some unidentified men in a car had forced her car off the road and shot her in the head.

I sat alone on the front seat of the bus, opposite the driver. I was hungry and exhausted. My fever was high and climbing. I didn't know it, but my cold had become bronchial pneumonia.

During the night, my brain became a whirl of nightmarish images and sounds. Whenever the driver would hit the brake or steer around a curve I would jerk awake, and in the highway ahead, in the beam of the headlights, I would see hooded Klansmen standing.

Maybe I talked or made a noise. One of the other passengers came forward and sat by me. He was a burly, white-bearded man, about 55 or 60 years old. He spoke with an Irish brogue. His name was Tim Murphy, he said. In his youth, he was in the Irish Republican Army, and had fled to America in 1923, a fugitive from the British. He was a labor organizer for the Longshoremen's Union on the New York waterfront.

"Some young man should have climbed to the top of the capitol and raised the Stars and Stripes," he said. "That wouldn't have been very nonviolent, though." He talked all night of Ireland and ancient kings named Brian.

At midnight on March 27, we arrived in New York. Roy and Bob and I were supposed to board another bus immediately and continue on to Boston. "Don't go," Tim Murphy said. "Come have a drink with me. There's another bus in two hours." Roy, a teetotaler, declined and boarded the bus for Boston, but Bob and I accepted. Mr. Murphy took us to an Irish bar near the waterfront. "Now you're ill," he said to me. "You must do as I tell you." He ordered us corned beef sandwiches and shots of Irish whiskey and beer chasers. He paid for it all and proposed a toast: "To freedom."

He proposed the toast many times. Neither Bob nor I would remember how we got on the 2 a.m. bus to Boston. We slept all the way home.

March 1990

GOING WITH THE DAWGS

There are no fans so rabid as the followers of six-man football, partly because it's an exciting game to watch, and partly because it's played in towns where absolutely nothing else is going on. People have time to think long on it, and fine-tune their emotions. I know this because I played six-man football in the early 1950s for the Fort Davis Indians.

The tall blue letters on the water tower are beginning to fade but still can be read, even from the interstate:

STATE CHAMPS
1979-'80

At the foot of the tower, the fry cook at the County Line Cafe has just served up the day's last Ellis County Collider Burger and is cleaning his grill. The cafe occupies one end of the Milford One Stop, which also is a grocery store and a garage. The grocery store is empty of people, but the loud thumps and clangs echoing from the garage out back say that someone is trying to separate a flat tire from its rim.

Across the street at the Country Corner, a boy wearing a cowboy hat is pumping Fina unleaded into his Ford Ranger. He's the only soul in sight. The Ellis County State Bank and the Milford Cash Grocery have been locked up for the night.

They, along with the One Stop and the Country Corner, account for nearly all the commerce in Milford, so the parking spots along the sidewalks are empty. So is the street.

At six o'clock on the first evening of September, the sun is still high and brutal and the school year hasn't started yet. But 200 of Milford's citizens (a sign on the edge of town says "About 700 Friendly People Plus 3 or 4 Old Grouches" live here) have come to Horton Field, "Home of the Mighty Bulldogs," to watch the beginning of their autumn.

They're sitting in lawn chairs and on parked cars along the sidelines, and in the bleachers along the north side of the field. Behind them, beyond the rows of parked cars, on the lawn of Milford School, little children have started a football game of their own.

On the west end of the field the Gordon Longhorns are warming up, and on the east end, the Milford Bulldogs. They've been warming up a long time. Coach Kevin Ray and his assistant, Brad Lane, glance nervously at their watches. "The officials are late," Coach Ray says. "If they don't get here soon, the coaches will have to referee."

The people leaning on the cars and sitting in the bleachers cast appraising eyes on the hometown boys, and on Coach Ray and Coach Lane, hoping for omens of greatness. "Get 'em, Dawgs!" they cry.

It isn't to be a real game, only a scrimmage. The first real game is still two weeks and 200 miles away, against Moran. But the Milford cheerleaders — Shelia, Robin, Kellie, Renee, Taree, Rachel, Beth and Jennifer — are dolled up in dress uniform and already in full cry.

"Oh," says Ron Scott, Milford's sixth-grade teacher and most vocal fan, "you come out here on an October night when it's just cool enough to wear a little light jacket, and the old moon is so bright, and every fan knows every player, and every daddy's rooting and every mama's rooting and every girlfriend's rooting, and the boys are playing their hearts out . . . Well, it doesn't get any better than that. No time. Nowhere."

A red station wagon turns off the highway. The officials have arrived. The Bulldogs and the Longhorns take the field. The trill of the referee's whistle pierces the air.

> Last year or thereabout
> It turned into a rout,
> With a score of zero to fifty.
> Since we won the game,
> We are proud to proclaim
> That beating Moran was nifty!

In Milford, winning is a strong tradition. Back in 1978, the Bulldogs lost only one game. That was to the Cherokee Indians — the eventual state champions — in the quarterfinals. Then they played two undefeated seasons and won back-to-back state championships in 1979 and 1980. They've made the state playoffs four of the past five years. Last year, May beat them, 54-20, in the quarterfinals. Then Zephyr beat May, 54-36, in the semifinals. Then Fort Hancock clobbered Zephyr, 76-30, for the state title.

Indeed, Zephyr got 45-pointed, a numbing humiliation in a championship game.

Maybe you haven't heard of Zephyr or May or Fort Hancock. Maybe Milford is just a sign on I-35E between Waxahachie and Hillsboro and a water tower in the distance. And you never read in the sports pages of Jamie Aguilar of Fort Hancock, Matt Mann of Higgins, Darrell Paul of New Home, Lewis Knapp of Trent, Bryan Keith of Zephyr or Bud Venable of Bovina, even though they made the All-State Team last year. None of them will make the pros. It's almost certain that none will play on a college team. It's unlikely that they even will be recruited.

And if you don't know about getting 45-pointed, well, you don't know about six-man football.

Coach Ray didn't know, until he graduated from college about five years ago and needed a job. "I'd never seen or heard of six-man ball," he says, "but I was offered the coaching job at Blum, and I took it sight unseen. I fell in love with the game. It's better fit for smaller, quicker kids than 11-man is. And you have to be in better condition to play it. There's a lot more running, and most of the players stay on the field longer than in 11-man.

"A big, strong, slow guy who might be a star 11-man lineman ... well, in six-man he'd just be slow. The other team would run around him like he was a rock."

The game was invented in 1934 by Stephen E. Epler, the coach at Chester High School in Nebraska, who was trying to figure a way for tiny schools with not many boys to play football. The schools in Coach Epler's neck of the prairie must have been *really* tiny. When the world's first six-man game was played on Sept. 26, 1934, four schools had to contribute players to put two teams on the field. Chester and Hardy Highs battled Alexandria and Belvidere Highs to a 19-19 tie.

The team that Coach Epler devised consists of a center, two ends and three backs. Most of the game rules are the same as for 11-man football, but with some important differences.

A six-man football field is 80 years long and 40 wide, not 100 long and 50 wide. The goal posts' uprights are 25 feet apart, not 23, and their crossbars are nine feet high, not 10. Each quarter of play is 10 minutes, not 12. The ball must be moved 15 yards for a first down, not 10. A field goal counts four points, not three, and the scoring for extra points is reversed — a kick is worth two points, and a run or pass is worth one.

Also, the quarterback — or whoever takes the ball from the center — can't run across the line of scrimmage with the ball unless he hands off to another player and then receives it back. Also, any member of the team is eligible to receive a pass.

These rules, plus the sparcity of bodies on the field, make for fast, wide-open, razzle-dazzle play, full of options, end-arounds, reverses and faked punts and field goals. It isn't unusual for the center to catch a touchdown pass. It isn't unheard-of for the center to *throw* one — to the quarterback. High-scoring games are usual, replete with 60-yard runs and 70-yard passes, lacking the piles of bodies at the line of scrimmage that characterize 11-man football.

"I tell my friends in Dallas, if you want to see some *real* football, come down to Milford on a Friday night," says Max Kimrey, who lives in Milford and commutes to work in Mesquite. "Compared to six-man, regular football is plain boring."

Trent beat Panther Creek, 89-69, last year. Lazbuddie beat Wilson, 64-44. Strawn beat Newcastle, 52-47.

"The only time six-man is boring is when it's a real tight defensive game," says Joseph Calderon, a 1989 Milford graduate who has driven 75 miles from Tarleton State University in Stephenville to watch his old teammates scrimmage Gordon. "In the game for the district championship last year, we beat Covington, 22 to 20. That was pretty boring."

But scoring can get monotonous sometimes, too. Hence the 45-point rule: If a team has its opponents down by 45 points or more after the first half, the game is over.

"We played Moran last year," says Mr. Calderon, "and we had them 50 to nothing at halftime. They drove 200 miles down here and then had to leave after only 20 minutes on the field. Their coach told our coach, 'You've got to come to Moran next year. You'd better be there.' It was kind of a dare. He was pretty upset."

> *It will happen again,*
> *'Cause it's part of our plan.*
> *With our coaches, our players and staff,*
> *We will win in the end,*
> *But we'll still be friends,*
> *Even though we'll retire them at the half.*

According to the rules of the University Interscholastic League, which governs public school sports in Texas, only high schools with fewer than 100 students may compete in six-man football. A decade ago, 58 teams played it. This year there are 86 six-man teams, and their number is growing. "As the small towns of Texas get smaller, so do their schools," says Bob Young of the UIL.

Nearly all the six-man schools are west of I-35, in the barely populated vastness of the West Texas cattle and oil empire. Milford and the other schools in its district — Covington, Blum, Buckholts, Aquilla, Abbott, Bynum and Boles Home of Quinlan — are the eastern end of six-man country.

In the 1940s, Milford had seven churches, two cotton gins and 30 businesses. Most of them are gone now. The town's population hasn't shrunk as small as many of Texas' old farm communities, but it hasn't grown, either. About 800 people lived there at the end of World War II. Its official city limit sign says 664 live there now. One hundred ninety-three children attend Milford School. Forty-nine are in high school.

Seven of Milford's 10 football players graduated last spring, so Coach Ray and Coach Lane are constructing a new team around the remaining lettermen and a transfer from Waxahachie. "We don't have much experience," Coach Ray says, "but we have speed."

At 12:50 p.m. on the season's first game day, every Milford School student, from innocent kindergartener to worldly senior, gathers in the cafeteria to pump school spirit into the Bulldogs. The cheerleaders bounce and jump. The boys in the audience bark like bulldogs. The coaches and the two seniors on the team, James Claiborne and Carl Essary, deliver speeches promising great effort and victory. Ron Scott, whose custom-made poems have become a pre-game tradition at Milford School, reads his new work, "The Battle at Moran." The room quivers with cheers and laughter. The kindergarteners, seated on the floor at the front of the room, stare wide-eyed at the glory of it.

About 2 p.m., the players start loading the school bus for the drive to Moran, the longest trek the Bulldogs will take this season. "Oh, I love these trips to West Texas," Mr. Scott says. "You go so far out there you think you're going deer hunting, and you find the little bitty town — some of them don't even have a water tower — and you play the game, and then you get a couple of 99-cent hamburgers and a big Coke, and you get on the bus and come back home. That's what it's all about. It's fantastic! It's a thrill!"

"This is going to be a mad house," Coach Ray says. "Look at all this stuff. It's like we're going to camp." When the football equipment and cheerleaders' megaphones, coolers, duffel bags, makeup boxes and radios, eight cheerleaders, 11 football players, coaches, managers and sponsors are piled in, Coach Ray issues an official admonition — "I don't want you acting up and making a lot of noise. There's no call for that" — and at 2:30 the bus departs with Mr. Scott at the wheel.

Highway 22 to Hillsboro, then to Fort Worth via I-35W, then to Cisco via I-20, then to Moran via Highway 6. It's a long, long road, and hot. All the windows are wide open, but the breeze generated by the bus's movement is hot, too. The passengers settle down with books, magazines and Walkmans, and sweat.

At 3:30, Coach Ray hands out sandwiches and soft drinks. At 4:15, as if obeying some silent signal from nature, the eight cheerleaders simultaneously open their kits and launch a fluster of lipstick application, brushing and spraying of hair and painting of nails, beclouding the bus in cosmetic chemicals. At 5:15, Mr. Scott stops in Ranger for gas. Coach Ray declares the rest of the way to Moran a "quiet time," to "get our minds set."

The time and temperature sign at the Ranger bank says its 98. At 6:20, the bus pulls into Moran, population 335, and heads for the school at the foot of the town water tower. The players catch sight of the football field and gasp.

"God! Look at that! That's no field, it's a cow pasture!"

"They must have plowed that field, boy!"

"I'll bet they have rodeos on it!"

"Don't worry about the conditions," Coach Ray says. "Just think what you're doing. We're here to play football."

The field is a brown adobe brick of a place, strewn with rocks and a few sprigs of long-deceased grass, not of the kind usually grown on football fields, but the kind that the buffalo and longhorns used to eat. In both end zones and on the north sideline, where the visitors' cheerleaders will stand, are huge beds of red ants large enough to wrestle small puppies to the ground. A tangle of mesquite and prickly pear is threatening to swallow the visitors' bleachers, and there's no sideline bench for the visiting team.

A Moran school official explains to John Lilley, the Milford principal, that things are as they are because of a dearth of water and the electric company's unwillingness to erect a pole for a line to a pump that would bring water from a distant tank to the field. "We put up a new scoreboard and built a new fence and a new pressbox this year," he says. "We were hoping that's what you would notice. We plan to have a new field next year."

In the Milford dressing room, Coach Ray says, "I tell you what, guys. That out there is enough to make me want to go home at halftime."

At 7:30, when the announcer calls for the national anthem, Milford's eight cheerleaders and eight fans and the whole populace of Moran lift their voices, but they fade to a dry whisper under the sun, still a vicious disk high above the scoreboard. There's no flag on the pole the singers are facing, but after the anthem and the school songs are finished, someone goes into the school and gets one and raises it.

Milford kicks off, but after only a few plays Moran fumbles. Milford's Scooter Lynch recovers, and John Morgan later runs it in for a Milford touchdown.

But Moran is tougher this year. Clouds of dust rise from the field with each tackle. At the end of the first quarter, Milford leads only 6-2, and by the end of the half the score is only Milford 19, Moran 2.

Mercifully, darkness has fallen. The moon is high in the southwest. While the coaches pep-talk their teams at opposite ends of the field during halftime, the crowd watches two sparrow hawks chase bugs in the glare of the field lights.

Then John Morgan, standing near his own goal line, receives the opening kickoff of the second half and runs it all the way back for a touchdown. Moran, badly rattled, fumbles on its next possession, and Milford scores again. And again. And again.

"Atta boy, Dawgs!" Ron Scott cries. "You're looking mighty good from here!"

"Get with it, Dawgs!" somebody screams at the Moran team, which also is Bulldogs. "They're laughing at you!"

With 6:21 left in the third quarter, Milford leads, 40-2, and is only a touchdown away from 45-pointing Moran again. In the nick of time, though, Moran scores, and the third quarter ends with Milford leading only 40-8. Mr. Scott shakes his head. "We haven't won this yet," he says. "I've seen a lot happen in a 10-minute quarter."

What happens is Milford's Finel Brown passes to Ty Evans for one touchdown, and John Claiborne runs it in for another, and the game ends, 54-8, with 2:39 left on the clock.

The players, who have been on their feet for the whole game because there was no bench for them, shower and dress quickly and climb onto the bus. "Not so fast," says John Lilley, the Milford principal. "The locker room is a mess. That's not the way we want to be remembered here. Get back in there and clean it up."

Within half an hour of the game's end, the bus is back on the highway. It passes through a silent Cisco, where the bank sign says it's 10:30 and 95 degrees, and on to Eastland and a stop at MacDonald's for cheeseburgers and fries and Cokes. "Mind your manners," Mr. Scott tells the kids as they step off the bus. "Remember, you *are* the best."

Then it's on and on through the night, the kids chattering, bass thumping like heartbeats from the low-turned radios, 18-wheelers roaring past the open windows, the breeze cooling, oh, so slowly. Mr. Scott misses the turn from I-20 to I-35W, and picks his way down some two-lane alternate route past sleazy bars and adult video stores somewhere in Fort Worth, through half a dozen darkened little towns, vaguely southward. The kids gleefully jeer his mistake, and sing songs, and at last, near Waxahachie, only 20 miles from home, they fall asleep.

When the bus stops in front of the Milford School gym, they fumble for their belongings, stumble out the door, mumble muffled goodnights and disappear into the darkness toward their cars and homes. It's three o'clock.

"This was not a trip," Mr. Lilley says. "This was an odyssey."

October 1989

HANGING IN

From the mid-1970s to the mid-'80s, the skyline of downtown Dallas changed almost daily. I would be driving to work in the morning and see a skyscraper that I could swear hadn't been there the morning before. The civic tub-thumpers were bragging that the state bird of Texas was the construction crane.

Of course, to make way for all those shiny new towers, the developers were buying up and tearing down the more modest structures that had been downtown Dallas. And when the bust came and the construction crane migrated elsewhere, they left vacant lots and empty, decaying buildings where small businesses once had thrived. Still, a few survived.

"I'LL TELL YOU A STORY YOU CAN TELL YOUR GRANDCHILDREN SOMEday," Basil Sideris was saying. "There was a little newspaper lady, by name Margaret. This is a true story. You remember Margaret, the old newspaper lady, Frank? She used to work up and down?"

Mr. Sideris' friend, Frank Foster, nodded. Mr. Sideris' only customer at the moment, he was eating meat loaf and drinking Coca-Cola from one of those old-fashioned little 6½-ounce bottles.

"Margaret was about 80 years old," Mr. Sideris was saying. "She had two newspaper stands. One by the Baker Hotel and one in front of Neiman's. At these stands was a stack of newspapers and a brick to hold them down and a cigar box on the top. Are you listening? A cigar box on the top.

"The old lady would go around from one corner to the other and collect her nickels. She would leave the papers and the cigar boxes there all night, and in the morning she would find the right number of nickels in the boxes for the number of papers that were gone."

Mr. Sideris stabbed his finger toward his listener. "Now *that* was the city of Dallas," he said. "That's why I was so captivated. I thought, 'This is a paradise. I've got to stay here.'"

That was in the 1950s, he said, not long after he and his older brothers, Harry and George, and their mother had immigrated from Greece.

"Now," he said. He waved his arms toward the street, half in defiance, it seemed, half in resignation. "Now the newspaper boxes are locked and embedded in concrete. So there is the difference in what the city of Dallas used to be and what it is now."

The restaurant in which Mr. Sideris and Mr. Foster were sitting is in the basement at 1602A Main St. The Greek who opened it in 1936 and the Greeks who succeeded him called it the Pirate's Cave, and the floor mosaic at its entrance still says that. When the Sideris family bought it in 1958, they renamed it the Town House Deli, and that's what the sign over the doorway says. "But naturally, with three Greeks here and people coming in and saying, 'How's the Greeks today?' everybody started calling it 'The Greeks,'" Mr. Sideris said. "That's pretty much what it's been." So the wind-battered sign over the sidewalk just says: GREEK RESTAUR . . .

"Main and Akard used to be the heart of downtown Dallas," Mr. Sideris said. "We used to have customers from 10:45 until two o'clock in the afternoon continuously. Not anymore. The buildings around us are only about 25 percent occupied. The building next door has been vacant since 1968. A nine-story building. We have nothing but bums, hoboes and thieves downtown now. Women are afraid to walk on the street. When you open up in the morning and you find a bum sleeping in your doorway, that's not good news. Right or wrong?"

Mr. Foster, who is retired, said he wouldn't have been downtown on this particular day himself if he hadn't had to pick up some income tax forms.

"Our lease is up in December," Mr. Sideris said, "and that will be the end of this establishment. After 55 years. But a thousand years from now, when my ancestors and I are sitting around talking, I can tell them that I remember what the city of Dallas used to be."

What American city hasn't experienced the relocations and dislocations, the ruptures and realignments that Dallas has endured during the past few decades? Construction of freeways and suburban growth, proliferation of shopping malls, white flight from old neighborhoods, the switch from passenger trains and downtown stations to jet planes and outlying airports have changed all our urban landscapes. Many American downtowns simply have been abandoned, slowly, building by building, block by block, to rot and poverty and crime.

But Dallas was different, it once seemed. Fifteen years ago, Texans native and naturalized were bragging of the state's "recession-proof" economy. "Land, oil and agriculture," they used to say. "Texas' biggest businesses, and three things the world can't do without." They smiled at the problems of the worn-out cities of the so-called "Rust Belt" and boosted Dallas as "the city that works."

The price of oil would never fall, the common wisdom averred. "They aren't going to make any more land," the real estate agents said. The boom, presumably, would last forever. So downtown Dallas wasn't abandoned. It was torn down and rebuilt as the skyscraping business capital of an expected new order.

"As they tore down the old buildings, they replaced them with buildings with no space for small businesses," said Dee Watson, a barber. "Nothing but marble lobbies and potted plants. So the old ma-and-pa businesses disappeared."

Then the building boom stopped. Overnight, it seemed, the construction cranes disappeared from the downtown skyline. Speculators and developers who were caught owning old structures that hadn't yet been replaced with new glass towers tore them down and paved their lots for parking, or simply left the old hulks vacant, abandoned to rats and cockroaches, to wait out the bust.

Here and there, however, remain small survivors of what downtown Dallas used to be, before the boom, before the vast in-migration from the North, before the knock-down-and-build frenzy of 1976-85, before the financial disaster that followed.

Some are still hearty, some weak and fading, but all are vestiges of a different time, when Dallas was just an ambitious burg on the prairie, a bigger-than-most Texas town, full of businesses that were run by the families who owned them.

The Oriole Barber Shop, where Dee Watson cuts hair, was established by Walt Davis in 1912. As he aged, he hired a second barber, Doyle Watson, and later made him his partner. When Mr. Davis retired — he was in his 80s — Mr. Watson took over the shop. And when *he* retired — also in his 80s — he turned the shop over to his son, Doyle Jr., called Dee.

For decades, the Oriole and its owners had to dodge the wrecking ball. Dee Watson's recital of their odyssey is a history in capsule of the Dallas boom and the bust that followed:

"Mr. Davis had the shop originally where the old First National Bank Building stands on Akard today. That's where it stood from 1912 until '56 or '57, when they tore that area out and built First National, which was InterFirst and then First Republic and now is NCNB, but not the main one.

"We moved to where Sanger-Harris used to be, which became Foley's, which is empty now. When they tore our building down to build Sanger-Harris, we moved to where ThanksGiving Square is. We were there until '72, when they tore down the building to build that. We went over to where Dallas One Center is now, which is where the old Cullum Building used to be, then I moved over on Elm to the 1900 Pacific Building.

"They didn't tear down that building, but they renovated back when they thought everything was going to keep being rosy, and they tripled the rents. They went from $12.50 to $35 a square foot. I said, 'Bye' and came over here."

The Oriole Barber Shop proved hardier than most of the banks and corporations that evicted it. It's at 1926 Main St. now, just down from the police department, where, Mr. Watson said, business is good, but not as good as it used to be. He waved his comb toward the square-block-big empty building across the street.

"When the Joske's store closed down, 800 employees disappeared." He waved toward the empty 32-story Mercantile Bank Building — or is it the MBank Building or the Momentum Bank Building? — in whose shadow he cuts hair and dusts his customers with talcum powder.

"You have to have a reason to come downtown," he said, "and they've taken it all away. The developers drove out all the stores. Even if you come down here, you have to pay to park, then if the meter runs out, they tow you away or ticket you, and if that doesn't happen, you get mugged before you get wherever you're trying to go.

"Some mornings I come to work and walk down this street, and I kind of wonder why I'm coming down. But the shop will be here as long as I can keep going. My dad worked downtown until he was 80. We've had a connection with downtown Dallas all his life and all mine, too. I tell you, though, it's nothing like it used to be. Not at all."

A couple of blocks away, at 2206-08 Elm St., Don Cowan, Jr., owner of Wald's Police Supply Co., said he intends to stay on the spot where his business was established by Sol Wald in 1935 because downtown is where his customers — city, county, state and federal law officers — are. "This is a competitive business, supplying police officers and security people," he said. "Being downtown gives me a little edge, I think."

But even though his store is full of rifles, shotguns, handguns, ammo, bulletproof vests, gas masks, riot sticks and off-duty cops doing their shopping, Mr. Cowan recently installed a buzzer lock on his front door. "Within the last year, the people who come in off the street, who apparently are living on the street, have gotten more aggressive," he said. "We felt we needed a way to screen people coming in. It's not a crime thing. They're just homeless folks. If you choose to be downtown, they come with the territory. It's not like it used to be down here."

"Used to be" is the recurring theme in the talk of those who have worked downtown a long time. Maybe their memories are rosier than the past really was — time fades the bad days first, it seems — but they're vivid and warm and honest. They tell stories — some handed down through generations — of a smaller, safer, more manageable city, where movie stars, generals and presidents used to arrive at Union Station on trains and check into the Adolphus Hotel, of oil and cattle and cotton people who used to come from the boondocks and blow thousands of dollars on whirlwind shopping sprees.

"One cold Christmas, this huge gentleman walked into the store," said Lewis Novin, whose father founded Novin's Jewelry as a Deep Ellum pawnshop in 1906.

"The gentleman had sold a lot of his cattle to one of the yards that used to be out north of Dallas. His feet were muddy and covered with manure. He had walked into one of the major jewelry stores, and they almost ran him out. So he came into ours, and he was feeling pretty good, and he said, 'I want to buy myself a *biiiig* diamond.' We happened to have a big yellow one in the window. I showed it to him, and he liked it.

"Well, he wore a size 14 ring! That's four or five sizes bigger than the average man's finger! He growled, 'If you'll get it ready for me right away, I'll take it.' The price was $3,000. Thirty years ago, $3,000 was a lot of money. I measured his finger with a piece of string and called my repair shop and told them not to close yet. The gentleman started pulling out the checks he had gotten for his cattle, and he endorsed one and said, 'I think this one here will cover the ring.' It wound up being a beautiful Christmas."

The store later relocated to Main and St. Paul streets, where the Novins' $200 monthly rent remained the same for 40 years. "I used to walk from our store up to the Mercantile Bank, which is deserted now," Mr. Novin said. "I knew every little merchant all up and down the street. The tailor shops, the florist shops, the cafes, the barber shops. Today they're not even there. They've closed up whole blocks."

When the air conditioning went out a few years ago, the new owner of Mr. Novin's building thought it better not to renew the leases of his tenants and closed down, rather than install a new system. Novin's Jewelry moved again, to 1907 Commerce St.

They still repair watches there — the kind with gears and springs and balance wheels. Or, if you're down on your luck or need a few bucks to tide you over until payday, you can hock the watch.

"Since we've been in this new location, our pawn business has increased about 20 percent a month," Mr. Novin said. "We're close to the post office, we're close to the federal building, we're close to NCNB. You know, these banks won't make small loans anymore, even to their own employees, so when they need $50 or $100, they come in here."

Novin's is what he calls an "envelope pawnshop." It accepts only jewelry. "Everything we loan money on goes into an envelope and into the vault," he said.

If it's a gun or a musical instrument or a set of tools that the bank employee wants to offer, he might try Label's Pawn Shop at 2038 Commerce, where the company motto on the business cards is: "If Not Able See Label."

Its present address, just west of Central Expressway, is the third for the shop since Lewis and Sylvia Label founded it in 1946. "We used to be on Elm Street," Mr. Label said. "All the pawnshops were on Elm Street then. We called it Elm Street Row. But it's all gone."

"Nearly all the buildings at this end of town are empty now," Mrs. Label said. "And there are 100 pawnshops in Dallas County, out in the suburbs, where people live. Why would they come down here? But we've had our customers for years and years. Some of our customers now are grandchildren of our customers from the old days. They know us. If they call and ask us to hold their pawn a little longer so they can redeem it, we do. Most pawnshops won't. Ninety days and it's gone."

Everybody knew each other. That's what they all say. "We were on a first-name basis," said Bernard Hirsh. "In the olden days, we had all those little shops — hat shops, shoe shops, dress shops, drugstores, fruit stands, lunch counters — and I knew everybody. It was exciting to walk down the sidewalk. Now there's nothing left. It's not fun like it used to be. For me, at least."

Yet, entering the store that Mr. Hirsh owns and runs with his son Robert, you could think that nothing at all had changed. Not in 50 years. Not in 75. Milliners Supply Co. at 911 Elm St. looks much as it did when its founders, Martin and Charlotte Weiss, opened their business at this same spot on or about St. Patrick's Day, 1911.

Rolls of ribbon, packets of beads and sequins, showcases full of cloth flowers and jeweled tiaras, hats of every color, boas and plumes, and feathers of ostriches, turkeys and pheasants line the long, narrow building from end to end. The showcases, built of dark, indestructible wood and topped with thick, beveled glass, were purchased second-hand from A. Harris & Co. — predecessor of Sanger-Harris, predecessor of Foley's — in 1914. So were the ranks of long, dark, wooden drawers, containing who knows what, that line the walls. The wooden counters near the back are intricately scarred by almost a century of scissors snipping bolts of lace and netting. The wooden floor is worn by 80 years of women's shoes. The huge brass cash register, festooned with molded baroque curlicues, bought new from National Cash Register when the store was opened, is still in use. A computer and a fax machine, incongruous, sit beside it. "I haven't yet found a computer table that works in with our furniture scheme," Robert Hirsh said. The Hirshes, father and son, work at roll-top desks. On the wall behind the cash register, Martin and Charlotte Weiss — uncle and aunt of Bernard Hirsh's late wife, Johanna — gaze somberly from oil portraits in gilt frames.

The Weisses, who had operated a general store in Beaumont before they moved to Dallas, opened the business to sell supplies to the city's booming hat industry. "Dallas was the fourth largest millinery center in the United States, after New York, Chicago and St. Louis," Bernard Hirsh said. "We had 33 hat factories when I entered the business in 1945. Now there is one.

"Women just don't wear hats anymore, because of bouffant hair-dos, low cars and a new way of life — athletic clothes, exercising, running, jogging. They just don't want to bother with hats anymore. So most of our merchandise is wedding merchandise now. Headwear and accessories, things that can be put on something or with some-thing. We publish a catalog, and most of our business is mail order now — bridal shops, fabric shops, department stores, craft shops — all over the country."

"We don't get to meet our customers very often," Robert Hirsh said. "That's the bad thing about it."

On shelves in the store's upstairs storage area, dozens of wooden hat blocks — used in the '30s, the '40s, the '50s to mold women's hats out of felt — sit row on row. Bernard Hirsh bought them years ago from going-out-of-business hat factories. "To me, each of them is a treasure, a work of art," he said. "Each one is hand-carved, each has a different personality, each is unique."

When Martin and Charlotte Weiss opened their shop, the Blue Front Restaurant — established in 1877 — already had been in business for 34 years. When W.G. Schliepake bought the restaurant in 1929, it was open to men only.

During the Great Depression, however, Mr. Schliepake laid off his waiters and brought in his family to help him — first his wife, Anna, in 1932, and later his son, Willie, and his daughters, Lena, Annie, Frances, Pauline, Louise, Josephine and Eva Kathryn. "Mama helped turn it into a family restaurant," said Louise LeCour, who, with her sisters Eva Kathryn LaCoke and Josephine Wellbaum, still runs the place. "She made women and their kids feel at home."

Willie, Frances and Annie are dead. Pauline lives in Shawnee, Okla., and hasn't worked at the Blue Front for many years. Lena is retired, after working for 63 years. She's 88 years old now. "Nobody leaves here until they just cannot work anymore," Mrs. LeCour said.

When Louise, Josephine and Eva Kathryn were young, they used to sing as a trio called the Swingettes. They traveled about the country on a bus with the Durwood Klein Orchestra, and sometimes they would sing for the diners at the Blue Front. "Mama used to say, 'Sing, children,' until we were up in our 40s," Mrs. LeCour said, "and everybody loved it."

The Blue Front's original building at 1105 Elm St. was torn down to make way for the First International Building, which became InterFirst II, which became Renaissance Tower during the years of Dallas' Incredible Disappearing Banks.

"Then we were at Field and Commerce, under Jack Ruby's Carousel Club for two years — I went up there one time, before I was married — and then to the Underground in 1973," said Mrs. LeCour, referring to downtown's system of tunnels connecting office buildings. The restaurant's official address is 1310 Elm St., just two blocks from its place of origin. "Everybody that's anybody in Dallas has eaten at the Blue Front. The newspaper people. The judges. The lawyers. When they walked into the Blue Front, they were just folks. We knew everybody. There was hardly a stranger came in. We introduced them to each other and sat them down together."

The Blue Front opens at 6:30 every morning for breakfast. "Men like to come in and have their coffee and read their papers," Mrs. LeCour said. "They all sit at the same tables every morning." It used to stay open until 8 p.m., but several years ago, "when downtown became nothing but office space," Mrs. LeCour said, the sisters began closing the doors around four.

They shortened their extensive German menu, too, but there's still no lack of the basics: wiener schnitzel, bratwurst, Hungarian goulash, Irish stew, Polish sausage, sauerkraut, boiled potatoes . . . "We don't sell as much smoked tongue and pig knuckles as we used to," she said. "They were considered delicacies in the old days. People don't know much about them anymore." But they're still available.

When Robert Folsom was mayor, he proclaimed Oct. 22, 1977, to be Blue Front Day in Dallas, in honor of the restaurant's centennial, and Mrs. LeCour believes the photographs of the Schliepake family and their old restaurant at 1105 Elm will be hanging on the wall for a considerable time yet to come. "We're doing as well as anybody else downtown," she said. "We'll be around as long as you need us and one of us can make it down here."

"Used to be," Bob Walker said, sounding the theme again, "every block had two or three barbecue stands, and everybody was real busy. Then they started putting snack bars inside the buildings to keep the people from taking a lot of time on breaks. We used to sell 700 to 800 cups of coffee a day. But that's all gone now."

Mr. Walker's father-in-law, J.T. Bell, opened Bell's Barbecue 56 years ago. Thirty-six years ago, Mr. Walker started working for him, and two years later married both Mr. Bell's daughter and his business. In 1958 they moved their wood-burning barbecue pit to 1215 Jackson St., where it has been ever since.

"When we first opened here," Mr. Walker said, "WFAA was just across the street, and they had the *Early Bird Show*. They had live musicians, and they would come in here in the morning and lay down their guitars and bass fiddles and drums, and when it was time for them to go on, they would go across the street and play, and I could hear them on the radio."

The block used to be in the midst of Dallas' garment district, which moved years ago out to Stemmons Expressway, and Bell's was next to the back door of the Carousel Club. From time to time, the strip joint's not-yet-famous owner, Jack Ruby, would come in for a sandwich.

"He never did sit down," Mr. Walker said. "He would just walk around and eat barbecue and talk."

Today the barbecue stand occupies the ground floor of a parking garage between Bell Plaza and the rear of the Earle Cabell Federal Building. Its metal chimney rises past six stories of cars to spread its aroma over the neighborhood like a blessing. On the other side of the block, residents of the Manor House — one of the few buildings downtown in which people live — open their windows to catch whiffs of the smoke. "We get quite a bit of business from over there," Mr. Walker said. "And we're lucky enough to be sandwiched in between the telephone company and the federal government. They look to be fairly stable. At least the telephone company does."

Over at 108 North Akard St., at The Oyster House, Lucille Mathews remembers Jack Ruby, too. She started waiting tables downtown in 1954, first at the Royal Grill, then at Club 22, beneath the Carousel, then for 21 years at Sol's Turf Bar.

The building that Club 22 and the Carousel occupied was torn down, along with the Baker Hotel, and replaced with Bell Plaza. Sol's and the Commerce Street News Stand next door — both were old downtown institutions — fell a few years later to make room for more Neiman Marcus parking.

"In the 1950s, there were nightclubs all along Akard Street and Commerce Street," Ms. Mathews said. "The people would be all dressed up and going to the clubs and having a time. Downtown was *the* place for night life then. Downtown *was* Dallas then, and the entire city was busy at night."

"Yeah, it's so different than it used to be," said Rusty Montgomery, who bought The Oyster House from Charlie Gambolis' wife, Sandy, 2½ years ago.

It opened on Main Street in 1924 as the Eat Well Restaurant. It was moved to its present location and named The Oyster House in 1965. A plaque on the wall, presented that same year by Dallas Power & Light, certifies that it occupies one of the first all-electric buildings in Dallas. Many years earlier, its spot was the coffee shop of A. Harris & Co., predecessor of Sanger-Harris, predecessor of Foley's.

Mr. Montgomery has added barbecue and a few other items to the old seafood menu, and Ms. Mathews continues to serve up the two-ounce drinks that have been an Oyster House attraction for 25 years. Mr. Montgomery said business has doubled since he bought the place.

"We're in the center of what is left of the financial district — the banks, the insurance companies, the oil companies," he said. "Lunch is mostly suit-and-tie, but the evenings are working people — the maintenance people, the security guards, the telephone operators. Crazy Ray, the Cowboys' mascot, drops in about three times a week and blows up balloons for the customers. And on Friday nights, when we're open till two and all the other places downtown close at eight or nine, all the waiters and waitresses congregate here and tote up the score, what all's been happening that day. Lucille loves it. Waiters and waitresses are very good tippers."

"Oh, yes," Ms. Mathews says.

At the Greeks' Basil Sideris was talking to Mr. Foster. "The old tradition used to be, 'a rolling stone gathers no moss,'" he said. "But now *only* a rolling stone gathers moss, which is money. You hear what I'm saying? You have to be where the people are to make money."

Mr. Foster nodded. "And the people left," he said.

"And we should have followed them," Mr. Sideris said. "Years ago."

March 1991

THE YEAR OF RECONCILIATION

To many Americans, the Indians are figures of the past, a brave and colorful race who impeded the conquest of the continent by the whites for a while, were finally defeated and have faded into history. But of course they haven't really faded. In many places the native cultures remain strong, and the ancient pride of the nations remains intact. Neither are the Indians' old troubles with the whites all dead. Long after the last sad bloodletting, hundreds of quarrels and disputes between Indian nations and their conquerers remain. In 1989 and 1990, when several Great Plains states were celebrating the centennial of their entrance into the Union, one governor thought his people should think about making peace as well.

SEVERT YOUNG BEAR'S AUNT WAS STILL A BABY WHEN SHE DIED. THE .45-caliber bullet ripped through her body and lodged in the shoulder of her mother, who was carrying the child on her back.

"Until 1926, my grandmother carried that bullet in her shoulder," Mr. Young Bear said, "the bullet that killed her baby."

Almost a century has passed since the baby died. The wounded grandmother, whose name was Smoke, has been dead for 43 years now. Her grandson is 56. But his voice was heavy with sadness as he told the awful story of the baby and the massacre at Wounded Knee.

"It is a very sad place," Mr. Young Bear said. "It is full of spirit."

Nearly 500 soldiers — including troops of the 7th Cavalry, the ill-fated unit led by Gen. George Armstrong Custer against the Sioux and the Cheyenne at Little Big Horn in 1876 — massacred more than 150 Indians on the bloody morning of Dec. 29, 1890.

It was the last significant clash of arms between Indians and the U.S. Army. And it established a legacy of racial mistrust and fear in the new state of South Dakota that has endured for a century.

Now, during the centennial year of the massacre, Gov. George Mickelson is trying to set South Dakota residents on a different track. Earlier this year, as South Dakota's celebration of its first century of statehood wound to a close, Mr. Mickelson called together the heads of the state's nine Indian tribes, smoked the pipe with them in the Capitol rotunda and proclaimed a "Year of Reconciliation" between South Dakota's 50,000 Indians and 665,000 whites.

It marked the first time that a South Dakota governor officially had recognized the pain of the Indians' past and tried to heal the rift between the two races.

"It's my guess that 70 percent of the white people in South Dakota have never been on an Indian reservation, and I would like for them to go take a look," said Mr. Mickelson, whose father struggled with the same tensions when he was governor 40 years ago.

The proclamation, which also was signed by the tribal chairmen, called on South Dakotans "to look for every opportunity to lay aside our fears and mistrust, to build friendships, to join together and take part in shared cultural activities, to learn about one another, to have fun with one another and to begin a process of mutual respect and understanding that will continue to grow into South Dakota's second hundred years."

Although the massacre remains an emotional issue — particularly among full-blood Sioux and the elderly who remember survivors — "reconciliation" has become an often-used word in public ceremonies and celebrations.

Mr. Mickelson has spoken frequently to white and Indian audiences about racial harmony. He appointed a Council on Reconciliation, composed of religious and civic leaders of both races, to promote local Year of Reconciliation events and projects around the state.

"Wounded Knee was in our first year of statehood," the governor said in an interview. "The death of Sitting Bull was in our first year of statehood. I believe as governor I have a responsibility to do something to start our second century better than our first. I hope the result of this Year of Reconciliation will be a change in the attitudes of the two races toward each other."

There are encouraging signs. The hospital at Fort Meade, which was a cavalry post at the time of the Wounded Knee massacre, has installed a stained-glass "Year of Reconciliation" window in its chapel, depicting a cavalryman and a Sioux warrior at peace with each other. The residents of Mitchell and the Lower Brule Sioux Reservation have established a "sister city" relationship.

Oglala Sioux Tribal Chairman Harold Dean Salway, addressing the annual Black Hills Powwow in Rapid City urged the Indians and whites in the audience to "put the past behind us and look toward the future."

"And let's face it together," he said.

Tim Giago, publisher of the weekly Indian newspaper, *Lakota Times* and a critic of government Indian policy and white racial attitudes, told the same audience, "I've seen changes between Indians and non-Indians in South Dakota that I thought I would never see in my lifetime."

But there are cynics and skeptics in both groups. In their 1990 election-year platform, South Dakota Democrats criticized Mr. Mickelson, a Republican who is running for a second term, saying he had a "shallow, hypocritical commitment" to reconciliation. They offered no race-relations program of their own. Many whites in the state simply do not like Indians.

"I see a lot of prejudice," said Duane Brewer, a member of the Oglala Tribal Council on the Pine Ridge Reservation. "People really hate the Indian. . . . When an Indian applies for a job, they look at your resume, and the first thing they ask you is, 'Do you have a drinking problem?'"

Mr. Brewer said many Indians think that the governor committed political suicide with the proclamation. But, he said, "There are a lot of Indians who have been waiting for this, for an attitude change on the part of the non-Indians. . . . Our Sioux religion teaches that you don't carry hatred in your heart, that you treat other people with respect."

Ironically, it was religion that precipitated the Wounded Knee tragedy. In 1889 in Nevada, a Paiute Indian named Wovoka declared himself the Messiah. He had come to the Indians this time, he said, because the whites had rejected and killed him. If the Indians would constantly dance a ritual that he called the "Ghost Dance," he soon would make whites disappear from the earth, resurrect the Indians who had died, restore the vast buffalo herds and remake the world into an Indian paradise.

The new religion won an enthusiastic following on the Sioux reservations and the approval of the most famous Sioux leader, Sitting Bull. The Ghost Dance inspired a hysterical fear among the Indian agents and white settlers, who mistakenly thought the Sioux were preparing for an uprising. The Army was sent to stop the dancing, and one military blunder led to another until Sitting Bull had been murdered in his home and the Wounded Knee massacre had been committed.

When the shooting stopped, the bodies of 146 Indians lay near Wounded Knee Creek. Of them, 44 were women and 18 were children. Most of the 84 dead Indian men were unarmed. An unknown number of Indians who tried to escape were wounded and died elsewhere. Twenty-five soldiers died, too, some of them victims of their own comrades' fire.

The soldiers herded the survivors to the Indian agency at Pine Ridge. That night, a blizzard struck, preventing the return of a burial party to Wounded Knee for four days.

When they returned, the troopers dug a long trench on the hill where the artillery had been and unceremoniously dumped the Indian bodies into it, along with the corpses of several horses and mules.

"The massacre was a planned thing," said Verlene Ice, Severt Young Bear's cousin, who lives a few hundred yards from the massacre site. "The soldiers wanted to kill us to get revenge for Custer."

Ms. Ice and Mr. Young Bear are among those at Pine Ridge who remain suspicious of whites claiming to be friends of the Indian. "It's just words," Mr. Young Bear said of the governor's Year of Reconciliation. "He has gone around the state smoking the pipe with all the chiefs. The pipe is sacred to us. . . . It isn't something you do lightly. But I think the governor is doing it lightly, for politics."

Mr. Young Bear acknowledges that his views sometimes are considered controversial, even on the reservation. "They call me a militant and a troublemaker," he said.

It was he who invited the militant American Indian Movement to Pine Ridge in 1973 to protest the murder of Mr. Young Bear's uncle, Yellow Thunder, just across the Nebraska line from the reservation, and the alleged reluctance of Nebraska officials to investigate the killing.

AIM turned the protest into a general denunciation of federal Indian policy.

Members of AIM and some local Indians, including Mr. Young Bear, invaded and took over the community of Wounded Knee and held off an army of U.S. marshals and FBI agents for 70 days before agreeing to a cease-fire. By the end of the siege, a number of Wounded Knee homes had been vandalized, a store and a church had been burned, two Indians had been killed, an FBI agent had been paralyzed and the tribe was deeply divided.

Mr. Brewer, the tribal councilman, was a lieutenant in the Indian police at the time. "I was hated," he said. "The AIM people called us 'goons.' We said 'goon' stood for 'Guardians of Our Oglala Nation.' I didn't think I would ever be accepted by my people again."

Many Indians say the AIM occupation and the attention that it received in the news media did more harm than good for the Indians.

"I've heard tourists in stores and restaurants ask for directions to the reservation, and the local people would tell them: 'Hey, don't go over there. They'll strip your car. They'll steal all your belongings. They'll kill you.'" Mr. Brewer said, "That's the reputation that we're going to have to overcome."

He believes that the tribe has some reconciling of its own to do, as well.

"There's a lot of tension between the full-bloods and the half-breeds. The full-bloods think the half-breeds are nothing," said Mr. Brewer, who is part white.

Frank Means, the head of a mineral studies program aimed at developing the tribe's mineral resources on the Pine Ridge reservation, believes that the Indians are partly to blame for white people's negative image of them.

"Our problem is that we've isolated ourselves. We've segregated ourselves out here on the reservation. We need to integrate, educate ourselves and find out about all these new technologies," he said. "But a lot of people say we would lose our customs and traditions if we did that. When I talk about these things, people think I'm nuts."

Among those who want to stay clear of the white man's way is Alex White Plume, a member of the tribe's executive committee, who called Mr. Mickelson's Year of Reconciliation "just plain silly."

"For 100 years the whites tried to terminate our tribes," he said. "They tried to assimilate us into mainstream society. But at the same time, they wouldn't allow us into their society because of racism . . . so we had to come back here and stay with our own people. As a result of that, our language has survived and our religion has survived. Our culture is coming back in leaps and bounds now."

Mr. White Plume said he was "on the road to assimilation" until AIM occupied Wounded Knee in 1973.

"When I was a kid and I went to see a John Wayne movie with other Indian kids, we cheered for John Wayne, against the Indians," he said. "But the occupation of Wounded Knee changed all that. The young people are proud to be Indian now."

Mr. White Plume suspects that the Year of Reconciliation is a scheme to trick the Indian tribes into giving up their sovereignty and their fight to regain ownership of the Black Hills.

If there is to be reconciliation between the races, he said, it must be done on the Indians' terms, not those of white society, and not the governor's. "If the governor wants to reconcile with the tribes, he's got to go all the way, not just part of the way. There have to be apologies made for all the massacres that were done to us, for all the awful things that were done to us over the last 100 years because of racism," he said.

But, Mr. Mickelson said, it is not in his power to "go all the way." Many of the problems and disputes that the Indians want solved — ownership of the Black Hills, hunting and fishing rights, gambling on reservations — are the federal government's responsibilities.

"I can't change the federal law," he said. "I can't solve problems that Congress is too gutless to deal with. But I can be an advocate for economic development. I can be an advocate for education. I can be an advocate for health care. And I can do what I can to change attitudes.

"I didn't grow up on or near an Indian reservation," he said. "And I came to this job fully believing . . . that I could solve all these problems in four months. I was totally naive. I didn't realize what a century of distrust had done. But we can start trying to put things right, and we ought to do it together."

July 1990

OLD FRIENDS

How many high school classes would attempt a 50th anniversary reunion? But the North Dallas High School Class of 1941 - the last class to graduate before World War II changed the world - always has considered itself special. After hanging around with its members all weekend, I did, too. I had as much fun as they did, listening to their memories of the way they were.

ARROW SHIRTS WERE ON SALE AT SANGER BROS. FOR $2 APIECE. SIRLOIN steak was 27 cents a pound at Safeway. Tyrone Power and Linda Darnell were starring in *Blood and Sand* at the Majestic and William Powell and Myrna Loy in *Love Crazy* at the Palace. *The Dallas Morning News* was promoting an upcoming series by Ernest Hemingway, who was "hobnobbing with Chinese, Japs, Britons, Russians . . . getting inside information on the ticklish Oriental situation." Royal Air Force fliers were training at Love Field.

Elsewhere, German bombs were falling on the grounds of Buckingham Palace, German U-boats were torpedoing American merchant ships in the North Atlantic, Nazi saboteurs reportedly were awaiting word from Hitler to destroy the Panama Canal, and while Mrs. W.P. Zumwalt of the school board was handing out diplomas to the graduating seniors of North Dallas High School, the Royal Navy was sinking the battleship *Bismarck*.

Bombs wouldn't fall on Pearl Harbor for six months yet, but the seniors of June 1941 already knew they were stepping into an extraordinary time. "We knew we were going to war," says Archie Hunter. "Some of the guys had skipped their senior year and had gone on and enlisted. Some of us went in right after Pearl Harbor. Some went to college for a year or two first, but nearly all of us got into it eventually."

Mr. Hunter is a member of the committee planning the 50th anniversary reunion of his class. He's sitting at a table at El Fenix restaurant in downtown Dallas on a sunny day in May, talking over plans with two other members of the committee, Erwin Hearne, an artist, and Alfred Martinez, the owner of the restaurant. They and Maurine Martin McAlister, who keeps track of the addresses and doings of their classmates, are the core of the group that has kept the spirit of the 1941 North Dallas Bulldogs lively.

They've remained more closely knit than most high school classes, they say. Their first reunion was in 1966 in the Crystal Ballroom at the Baker Hotel, 25 years after graduation. Every five years since then, class members have traveled from all over Texas and both coasts and the Midwest to gather for a weekend of reminiscence and revelry.

"I happen to mention to people that we're having a high school reunion," says Mr. Hearne, "and they say, 'You're having a *what*? You've got to be kidding!' They just don't understand. Heck, we were so glad to see one another after the war. I mean, that was a *big* war, and a *tough* war on many of us. A lot of our class members were lost. Just the fact that we had survived . . . that had a lot to do with it."

It's to remember those first of their number to die, and all those who have died since, that they still get together, and to laugh again at themselves the way they were half a century ago, and the world they knew then, which has disappeared.

"Back then, most of us lived in the same neighborhood and went to the same grade schools together," Mr. Hunter says. "Back then, people stayed in place more than they do now. Some of us went all the way through kindergarten and grade school and high school together."

"In those days, they didn't have organized sports for grade school kids like they do now," says Mr. Hearne. "We made up our sand lot teams and played each other in the neighborhood."

"It was the Depression," Mr. Martinez says. "We didn't have a lot of money and didn't go many places. Everybody was in the same category."

Dallas was a city of 235,000 the year they graduated. Cotton fields rimmed Northwest Highway. Fort Worth was a long way off. Collin County was in another universe. And the corner of Cole and Haskell avenues, just beyond Oak Lawn, where the school has stood since 1921, was in North Dallas.

"It was a different place then," says Marylynn Newcom Wilhite. "Even as a child, you could go all over Dallas on the streetcar, and nobody would worry about you. I remember when I was nine years old, going downtown on the streetcar and shopping for my aunt at the old Titche-Goettinger."

Mrs. Wilhite and her husband are among almost 200 North Dallas Bulldogs — members of the class of '41, and smaller numbers of the classes of '40, '42 and '43 — roaming the lobby of the Colony Parke Hotel, drinks in hand, during the May 31 Friday night mixer, the reunion's opening event. She says she started going steady with John Connie Wilhite when he was a junior and she a freshman.

"And we're still going steady," he says.

"He left me and went into the Air Force, and I was stuck by myself here for the last year and a half of high school," she says.

When Connie got his pilot's wings in 1944, they got married, and the bridegroom went off to join the D-Day invasion. He liked the Air Force so much he stayed in for two more wars and retired a few years ago as a lieutenant colonel.

"I volunteered for Desert Shield," he says. "I called them, and they said they had recalled a few who had retired very recently, but no 67-year-olds yet. The war was over before they got to me."

Jody Lander, who graduated a semester behind Col. Wilhite, in January 1942, was president of his class and a football player. "Our team was kind of a joke," he says. "In the 1940 season, my last year, we won only one game. We beat Sunset, 7-6. They then went on to the state finals. I don't know how we managed to beat them."

"North Dallas never was strong in sports," says Nancy Hunter Gilmore. "We liked to say we were academically oriented." Mrs. Gilmore was so studious that she was double-promoted and graduated within half a year of her older brother Archie. "He didn't speak to me the whole time I was in high school," she says. "He was the meanest son of a gun in the world. But now he's just a doll."

All about the room, the Bulldogs are regarding each other with that chin-raised, eyelids-lowered, peering-through-bifocals gaze. The tags on their chests display their senior yearbook pictures alongside their names, and it's the young, smiling faces of 1941 that make the memories click into place:

"Ah! My goodness! Look who's here!"

"Is that really *you*? It's so good to see you!"

They speak of Saturday matinees at the Knox Street Theater and midnight shows at the Majestic, smoking cigarettes behind the rifle range in back of the school, skinny-dipping in the school pool during PE class, double-dating in the family's '37 Ford and parking in the moonlight on Flagpole Hill.

"The most precious memories to me are the school assemblies," says Mitzi Schaden Messier. "They were always big productions, and I just loved them. When the band would play *Deep Purple* I would cry. And Saturday night there was always a dance in somebody's home. We danced to the big-band sound: Glenn Miller, Tommy Dorsey, Frank Sinatra . . . "

Others recall hours without end spent in detention in Room 103, under the watchful eye of Miss Minnie Keel. "She was a fiery little redheaded woman," Erwin Hearne says, "and everybody gave her a hard time, rolling marbles down the aisle, setting wastebaskets on fire. She endured it well, though. She died a few years ago at 107 years of age."

"Remember how we would lay the fuse of a pack of firecrackers across a burning cigarette in the locker room, and then go off to class?" Billy Sempert says. "And the cigarette would burn down? And when we had been in class about five minutes, it would reach the fuse and set off the firecrackers? And how those teachers would run out into that hall, trying to find out what in the world had happened?"

Alan Myers, editor of the yearbook and staffer on the school newspaper, says he wasn't the mischievous type. "Due to my particular nature, I went through North Dallas High School kind of in a dream. The only bad thing I remember doing was when we were studying Browning in English class, and five or six of us played hooky one day to go down to the Browning Museum in Waco. That was my only deviation from the straight and narrow."

At a table at the edge of the hubbub, Caroline Cherry Shoemaker is holding court. She was a baton twirler and the drum major, and she has brought her scrapbook, full of pictures and newspaper clippings from her twirling days.

She has lived in Dallas all her life, she says, but this is her first reunion, because the planning committee didn't know her last name until now. "The others have seen each other every five years, but I don't know who these people are," she says. "A gentleman called and wanted to bring me tonight, and I didn't recognize him when he walked up the steps."

As they recognize her picture on her name tag, the men approach her with a kind of shyness, as they must have when they were boys. They shake her hand and speak to her in low, respectful tones. But the women greet her with gushes of enthusiasm:

"Ooooh! Caroline! I would never have recognized you!"

"Isn't she pretty?"

"Yeeeees! You're gorgeous!"

"I twirled a baton with fire at both ends," Mrs. Shoemaker tells a visitor, "and we were the first ones to wear short skirts. Before us, the skirts were below the knees. We had a good band. Our band was selected to lead all the bands one year from downtown Dallas to Fair Park, so of course I got to lead them all."

As she talks, her eyes are scanning the milling crowd. "It's strange when you're in high school, and you're a senior — remember? — and you're so in love and you've been going steady and you just know you're going to marry that boy and live together for 50 years and be happy. But you didn't marry him. I don't know if he's here tonight or not. I wouldn't recognize him. In the annual he took a whole page and wrote of his enduring love, he would never ever leave me, death do us part. He would marry me and we would be forever flying away. I started to bring that annual tonight, in case he was here with his wife."

Woody Brownlee and O.S. Castlen ran the Cole & Haskell Drug at the corner of those two avenues, just across the way from North Dallas High. The store had a soda fountain and a jukebox, so of course it was a Bulldog hangout.

During World War II, Mr. Castlen published a little newspaper called *Bulldog Bull*, which he mailed to all the North Dallas boys who were in the service, to let them know what was going on at their school and what was happening to their classmates.

When the war finally ended, he published his last edition, in which he wrote:

"There is one final tribute due and one most hard to express because words are too weak and undramatic when we come to consider those long rows of white crosses . . . How weak we living appear . . .

when we try to offer anything in comparison to those gallant ones. . . . So, to those white crosses in Africa and Europe, and on the Pacific's sandy atolls, we offer this promise: There will never be a final chapter ascribed to you. We will never speak the final word for you, but will refresh your memory in the coming generations and point you out to our sons and daughters as time lasts."

Under the headline "To Those Not Returning," Mr. Castlen listed the names of 87 North Dallas High School students who had been killed in action, eight who were still missing in action and three who were prisoners of war.

Robert Breault is standing with several others on the front steps of the high school in the cool June 1 morning, gazing across Haskell at the boarded-up building that used to be Mr. Castlen's store. "It was a wonderful place," he says. "I used to take my lunch money and start off my morning with an ice cream soda before school. And we would go back and play the jukebox and jitterbug after school."

Many of the group haven't stood on these steps since the night they graduated, but remembering the drugstore triggers memories of the other businesses that used to stand along the streets near the school: Abbott's Barbershop, Patricia's Beauty Shop, Dick & Don's Texaco, Lange Florist, the China Clipper Restaurant, Pat & Monty's Drive-In Grocery, Jack Jolly's Cleaners, Charlie Pittman's Barbecue Stand . . . "A root beer float was the greatest thing there ever was," Archie Hunter says.

Inside, M.O. Black, the school's current athletic director, has rescued from the basement several framed pictures of the old senior classes and has cleaned them up and stood them against the wall in the hallway. The grads crouch before them, searching out themselves and their friends.

Mr. Black says he's collecting pictures of North Dallas athletic teams from the past. He plans to have them enlarged and display them about the school. "So these kids today can see that this school once had a great tradition," he says. "Most of the high schools in Dallas have lost their sense of tradition. We want to bring tradition back to North Dallas."

Dr. Ewell Walker, 94 years old, father of SMU football great Doak Walker and the first coach that North Dallas High ever had, studies a display of old faculty pictures on the wall. "She's dead," he says, pointing. "And he's dead, and he's dead, and she's dead."

Jack Howell is roaming the hallway with his 1941 yearbook and a pen, asking his classmates to autograph their pictures. "I didn't get my annual until after we graduated," he says, "and I didn't have a chance to get anybody to sign it, so I'm getting them all to sign it now. When you get to the 50th anniversary, you throw all inhibitions out."

"Jack is having a ball with his little book," says his wife, Margery. "He'll recognize somebody and look at their picture in the book and say, 'Oh, my Lord, look how fat he is.'"

"There are only about five people here I would recognize on the street," says Bill Allen. "The rest are like strangers to me."

"I've been called John, Bill, one guy called me Stephen," says Erwin Hearne. "I just answer, 'Oh, yeah,' to whatever they call me."

They file into the auditorium and sing the North Dallas fight song and the alma mater, which is sung to the tune that 99 percent of all alma maters are:

> High above in stately beauty with their spirits true
> Wave our white and orange colors glorious to view.
> Lift the banner, raise it skyward; loud its praises sing.
> Love and honor to North Dallas we forever bring.

Hardy Brogoitti is emcee. "Fellows, do you remember the first box of Valentine candy you bought across the street at O.S. Castlen's Cole & Haskell Drug? And some of the fellows teased you about it, so you said it was for your mother? And it really was? What about the first time you skipped school and you prayed your mother wouldn't be home to answer the phone when Miss Bigbee called? Remember the day you drove your family's '35 Chevy to school for the first time, and you circled the school three or four times, and nobody even noticed you? Remember who gave you your first kiss, and where you were? I don't."

He introduces Oscar Rodriguez, the young current principal.

"The school has changed quite a bit," Mr. Rodriguez begins.

Of the 1,400-member student body, he says, 65 percent are Hispanic. Most of them are of Mexican descent, but there has been an influx of South Americans lately. Twelve percent are Asian — Vietnamese, Cambodian, Laotian — and their number is growing. Some of the new students are from Africa. "The last time we counted, we had 32 countries represented here," he says.

"But one of the things that hasn't changed is that kids are still kids. . . . And there are some of us who are trying to bring back some of the values that you learned here, values that create good citizens, which the world needs to survive. The weird, radical things that we're trying to bring back are things like punctuality and manners. We're trying to teach the students that they have to come to school every day, to prepare for going to work every day when they leave here. . . . "

Later, a photographer is trying to arrange the reunionists along the front steps for a picture. They lined up there for many a school picture years ago, and they're behaving now as they did then, fidgeting, talking, not paying attention to the photographer's pleas, making those bunny ears behind the heads of their friends.

"The place hasn't changed much," Mitzi Schaden Tessier says. "I walked in and felt right at home."

Along the walls of the Colony Parke ballroom that night are huge displays of pictures, newspaper clippings and memorabilia from 50 years ago. Faculty members, ROTC cadets, sports teams, clubs, cheerleaders.

The class of '41 stares in wonder and surprised recognition at the photographs of themselves when they were young. "Look at that. I had on cowboy boots," says Paul Pond, gazing at an old black-and-white snapshot. "Gollee, that's what I always wore." He laughs. "Oh, my. Gollee. Oh, gosh."

Chuck Arlington & His Orchestra open with a mellow rendering of the alma mater. Then the Rev. G.C. McElyeh — a cheerleader in high school and an Episcopal priest now — invokes the blessing of God, and, while the musicians continue softly playing the alma mater, he reads the names of the Bulldogs of '40 and '41 and '42 and '43 who have died since their graduation. It's a long list, requiring five minutes to read.

After a moment of silence, Jody Lander, the emcee, says:

"Reunions are a competitive sport. During the first reunion 25 years ago, we compared children, vacation homes, cars. And we regarded with envy and with glee the waistlines of our classmates, their hairlines and their wrinkles. We hated the streamlined and loved the slobs.

"But we come to the 50th reunion, and things have changed. The competition now is just being here . . . For showing up tonight, I salute you, Bulldogs."

Art Hill, "the Bulldogs' answer to Old Blue Eyes," sings *Sentimental Journey*. A troupe of Bulldog volunteers performs a series of slaphappy skits from *The Furlough*, the senior publication of the class of '41. Then Mr. Arlington and his men swing into *In the Mood*, and the boys and girls of '41 move to the dance floor and suddenly seem young again.

"1941 was a good year," says Dorothy Burton Sebastian, editor of *The Furlough*. "Things will never be that way again."

July 1991

WEST TEXAS

The editor of Westways, a magazine published in Los Angeles, called me. She was preparing a special issue on West Texas, she said, and wanted me to write an introductory essay. In 1,200 words or less, she said, she wanted me to explain "what and where West Texas is, and why it seems to get into people's blood." A daunting assignment, trying to explain West Texas to Californians, but I gave it a shot.

Years ago, I was driving alone from Boston, where I had been living, toward the place where I had grown up, in the Davis Mountains, in the farthest end of West Texas, which is called the Trans-Pecos.

The first days of my journey, past the cities of the East and Midwest, along the crowded interstates between close-together towns, had been hectic and noisy, and the farther I drove, the more urgently I felt my need to get to the Out There. By the time I cleared Dallas and Fort Worth, I was bone tired. My eyes were scratchy from too little sleep, my nerves tattered from too much coffee. I kept telling myself to get a room and rest, and I kept replying that I would, at the next town. But while the exits flashed by, I kept the car pointed into the sun.

It was somewhere west of Abilene that I felt myself changing. Suddenly, it seemed, I wasn't so tired. My eyes were still gritty almost to the point of pain, but my nerves were quieting, my muscles relaxing.

Then I noticed. The highway ahead was long and straight, and there wasn't another car in sight. The highway behind me was just as straight and just as empty.

I hit the brake and pulled onto the shoulder, cut the ignition, got out, and stood very still beside the car and listened.

The only sound was the ticking of the engine cooling. I wanted to get away from even that, so I walked into the desert, making my way carefully through the creosote bushes and the cactuses, trying not to kick the sharp white stones.

Fifty yards from the highway, I stopped beside a huge and very old mesquite. Its lacy leaves were moving, even though I could feel no breeze. In the distance, a single locust whirred the only sound in the flat, chalky land.

As far as I could see, on the land and in the vast, bright sky, clear to the horizon, I was the only creature. I felt absolutely alone and absolutely free, standing in the bright, empty, silent space.

I drove on to Big Spring or Colorado City or whatever the next town was and got a room and slept soundly for many hours, for I was back in West Texas at last.

To those who don't know or understand it, West Texas is a hot, dry, empty vastness, a kind of purgatory, or even hell. But for those who love it — who welcome aloneness and silence — it's the home of the soul, a place that could give birth to religions, as the hot, dry, empty Middle East did long ago.

Exactly where it begins depends on whom you ask. A practical, modern boundary is Interstate 35, which splits the state from the Red River to the Rio Grande, linking Dallas-Fort Worth, Waco, Austin, San Antonio, and Laredo. Fifty-nine percent of Texas lies west of that highway and its cities, but only 9 percent of its water and 12 percent of its people. To those who live east of the road, that dryness and emptiness are the very definition of West Texas.

Others mark the boundary in other ways. Fort Worth says the West begins there, and, psychologically, there's some truth to the claim. "Cowtown," as the city still is called, stands on the eastern edge of the cattle kingdom and the cowboy culture, that fragment of Texas that has been so glorified in fiction and film that most of the world thinks it's the only Texas there is. But Fort Worth has water and trees, and there are no tumbleweeds bouncing along dusty streets, as so many foreigners come hoping to find.

Some say West Texas — indeed, the whole American West — begins a few miles farther along, at the 98th meridian, the invisible border between the half of the country that gets more than 30 inches of rainfall a year and the half that gets less, which is the West. But there are trees here, too, and running streams and pretty, man-made lakes, and quite a number of people.

All these boundaries are too far east for me. In my mind, true West Texas begins at the eastern border of the Panhandle. If you extend that line straight down the map to the Rio Grande, the hunk of Texas on the left is West Texas. Here are few trees, no lakes, little green grass, and not many people. Here is where the weak among our ancestors died, and the strong won the land by such brutal toil and bloody conflict that they became as flinty and unyielding as the land itself. Here is where you begin to feel the space and the silence.

Even so, the parts of West Texas aren't much alike. The plains of the Panhandle — closer to Kansas than to most of Texas — are so flat that there's no land to see, only sky. This was the land of the buffalo and the Comanche, and of pioneer wives who were driven crazy by the constant wind.

Its space is so huge that strangers sometimes fear they're about to drop off the edge of the world. And the sky — the only scenery there is — may be empty as a bright, upside-down bowl or roiling with clouds, dark and terrifying, full of lightning and tornadoes.

South of the plains, West Texas becomes rolling prairie, and barren basins that were ancient sea beds, and great plateaus covered with mesquite and greasewood and cactus. It's a land of sheep and goats and oil wells and almost nothing else, all the way to the Rio Grande.

And beyond the bitter Pecos, in that broad arm that juts between the two Mexicos, West Texas is a land of rugged mountains that rise to 8,000 feet, where highland grasses and pinon pines grow high above the scorching desert floor.

Here, in the Davis Mountains and the Big Bend, the harshest and most magnificent region of all Texas, is where the Apaches once held sway, where the border between Texas and Mexico always has been a figment of the Anglos' imagination, where God is said to have dumped his left-over materials after he created the rest of the world.

The Trans-Pecos is almost as empty of people now as it was then, on the day God rested, except in its extreme tip. Where the Rio Grande has cut a pass through the mountains, El Paso — West Texas' only real city — lies, closer in both distance and attitude to Albuquerque and Tucson — and to Juarez across the river — than to its Texan sisters back east along Interstate 35.

Varied as West Texas is, its space and light and silence make all its children kin, and different from other Texans.

Once I was in Wink, a bleak little oil town in the midst of one of the ancient sea beds — a place as different from my mountain home as you're likely to find, yet only 100 miles away. I was visiting with a woman who had lived in Wink all her life. We were talking about Roy Orbison, the rock star, who had grown up in Wink and had left, and about the woman herself, who had grown up with Roy and had remained.

"There's not any place else where I really want to be," she said, squinting into the bright, barren landscape. "And I can't stand trees for very long. They get in the way of the sky."

I nodded. I knew.

September 1992